WHO'S YOUR SOURCE?

WHO'S YOUR SOURCE?

A Writer's Guide to
Effectively Evaluating
and Ethically Using
Resources

MELISSA M. BENDER AND
KARMA WALTONEN

broadview press

BROADVIEW PRESS – www.broadviewpress.com
Peterborough, Ontario, Canada

Founded in 1985, Broadview Press remains a wholly independent publishing house. Broadview's focus is on academic publishing; our titles are accessible to university and college students as well as scholars and general readers. With 800 titles in print, Broadview has become a leading international publisher in the humanities, with world-wide distribution. Broadview is committed to environmentally responsible publishing and fair business practices.

© 2020 Melissa M. Bender and Karma Waltonen

Library and Archives Canada Cataloguing in Publication

Title: Who's your source? : a writer's guide to effectively evaluating and ethically using
     resources / Melissa M. Bender and Karma Waltonen.
Names: Bender, Melissa, 1967- author. I Waltonen, Karma, 1975- author.
Description: Includes bibliographical references and index.
Identifiers: Canadiana (print) 20190218266 I Canadiana (ebook) 20190218290 I
     ISBN 9781554814848 (softcover) I ISBN 9781770487246 (PDF) I
     ISBN 9781460406809 (HTML)
Subjects: LCSH: Information literacy—Handbooks, manuals, etc. I LCSH: Bibliographical
     citations—Handbooks, manuals, etc.
Classification: LCC ZA3075 .B46 2020 I DDC 028.7—dc23

Broadview Press handles its own distribution in North America:
PO Box 1243, Peterborough, Ontario K9J 7H5, Canada
555 Riverwalk Parkway, Tonawanda, NY 14150, USA
Tel: (705) 743-8990; Fax: (705) 743-8353
email: customerservice@broadviewpress.com

For all territories outside of North America, distribution is handled by Eurospan Group.

Broadview Press acknowledges the financial support of the
Government of Canada for our publishing activities.

Canadä

Edited by Tania Therien

Book design by Chris Rowat Design

PRINTED IN CANADA

*For the people who taught us to write ethically and effectively
and to the students to whom we hope to pass that down.*

Daenerys Targaryen: I can't have children.
Jon Snow: Who told you that?
Daenerys: The witch who murdered my husband.
Jon: Has it occurred to you that she might not have been a reliable source of information?

Game of Thrones, Episode 7, Season 7, "The Dragon and the Wolf"

Contents

EIGHT   **Using Sources to Support and Develop Your Argument** 209

NINE   **Ethical Writing Is Good Writing** 233

Acknowledgements

In writing this book, we aimed to articulate many of the assumptions that professional and academic writers make about conducting research and working with sources—assumptions that remain mysterious to students because they largely go unspoken. Without the many students that we have worked with over decades, we would not have known which mysteries to unlock.

We likewise thank our most recent cohorts of students, who have comprised the first audience for *Who's Your Source?* They have read chapters and provided valuable feedback.

We thank our editor, Marjorie Mather, who recognized the value of this book before we'd written a single word, and our University Writing Program colleagues who inspire us year after year with their commitment to providing excellent educational experiences for undergraduates at the University of California, Davis.

We also thank our librarians, Roberto Delgadillo and Ruth Gustafson, who teach us so much while they guide our students; the many writers we mention in this book, who create such great examples of good writing; and our writing support group (OOF).

Melissa would also like to thank her partners, Joanna Oseman and Matthew Baker, who have supported her through this and many other writing projects.

Karma would also like to thank her family and her friends who are closer than family, and all of the students, peers, and teachers who gave so freely of their time, energy, and ideas along the way. Asking for help is hard—thank you for teaching this stubborn woman that it's always the best idea to do so.

Or, What *The Simpsons* Can Teach Us about Sources

In 1995, Lisa Simpson became a vegetarian after an emotional trip to a petting zoo. When she asked her school cafeteria to provide vegetarian options, she got in trouble. The Principal even visited her classroom. Although he said he wanted "an open dialogue," he had the students sit silently and watch a filmstrip: "Meat and You: Partners in Freedom," created by The Meat Council, as part of the "Resistance is Useless" series.

In the filmstrip, a famous actor (who's been in other filmstrips, like "Firecrackers: The Silent Killer"), Troy McClure, and a young boy, Jimmy, tour a slaughterhouse. We don't get to see inside the slaughterhouse, though we do hear the awful noises of meat processing after the cattle leave the feedlot, which McClure calls "Bovine University."

After Jimmy stops shivering from what he's just seen, he asks McClure if his friend who doesn't eat meat is "crazy." McClure says, "your crazy friend never heard of the food chain." An image of the food chain appears, with all of the animals, including poodles, camels, and squirrels, going into a human. The filmstrip then cuts to a "scientician" in a lab coat, who doesn't get to say more than "uh," before it cuts back to McClure. McClure speaks for the scientician, saying all creatures eat each other, ending with, "If a cow ever got the chance, he'd eat you and everyone you care about."

Lisa is outraged by the propaganda: "They can't seriously expect us to swallow this tripe!"

However, the Meat Council has donated literal tripe to the class, and the other students swallow both kinds, labeling Lisa as a "Grade A moron" and a "crazy" friend. (One student, Ralph, declares that he's going to attend Bovine University someday.)

This book is designed to help you be like Lisa.

We[1] know you wouldn't fall for this.

However, after reading this book, you'll be able to analyze *why* on an incredibly geeky level.

You'll be able to question the design of the images and charts (like the one showing the food chain in *The Simpsons*), to challenge the rhetorical choice of asking students to sit quietly in lieu of open dialogue, to call out the biased and improper authorities being cited (Troy, the "scientician," the Meat Council) and other fallacies like quick fixes, non sequiturs, and stacking the deck, and to wonder how firecrackers could be a "silent killer."

Essentially, this book teaches you how to do two things: find reliable, valid sources and use them effectively and ethically in your writing.

Finding and Evaluating Sources

"Meat and You: Partners in Freedom" is an extreme example, used in a satiric way, but people do fall for persuasive arguments disguised as informative ones. We have had students think that advertisements were unbiased government public service announcements, specifically thinking that the famous "Got Milk" campaign was created by the American government, because milk is good for

---

1 Here, we're using "we" because we're talking about us—the authors. In other places, we use "we" in a more general sense—like "we all fall for fallacies sometimes." We're also using "you" because we're addressing you as if we're in conversation, as we would with our own students in class. Many of the papers you'll be writing for classes will have a different audience and, therefore, require a more formal style.

you. The campaign was actually created for the California Milk Processors Board (and then licensed to other states).

Governments do create public service announcements, to remind us to buckle up, for example. In this case of "Got Milk," it's the people who profit from the product who created the ad for it (as is typical).

Using Sources

Karma had a student bring in a draft a couple of years ago for an upper division Writing in the Health Sciences class. The student was arguing that doctors should order more MRI tests; he said that the cost would come down if they did.

Karma argued with the student: that's not how medical tests work.

The student tried to explain the concept of supply and demand. Then Karma tried to explain that supply/demand doesn't really apply to medical costs. The more a drug is needed, for example, the higher the cost is likely to be in the United States, after all.

Karma said that if the student wanted to make that claim, he had to find a source; otherwise, she and the other readers wouldn't be convinced.

In the final draft, the student's paragraph making the claim was the same, except for a source's last name in parentheses at the end.

Who was talking? If information actually came from this source, then how could the paragraph stay exactly the same after adding it in?

Karma went to the works cited page and then opened her computer and read the "source," which was about how some injuries should be evaluated by MRI and others by CAT scans. No mention of cost was made.

The student failed the paper and came in to office hours to talk about it.

"I don't understand this comment. What does 'this isn't what your source says' mean?"

"It means that isn't what your source says."

"What?"

"Your source doesn't say anything about cost, much less the cost coming down."

"How do you know?"

"I read it."

"The whole thing?!?"

"It was only a few paragraphs."

"That's embarrassing."

"I bet."

It was more than embarrassing, actually. This student had shown he wasn't interested in knowledge—in research—in providing true information. He was willing to lie on two levels—first, to give his readers false knowledge (that supply and demand applies to medicine) and to falsify evidence to support his lie.

It's not just animated characters and students who run into problems evaluating the reliability of sources or make questionable decisions about how to use them. In spring 2012, Jonah Lehrer hit the nonfiction bestseller list with *Imagine: How Creativity Works*, but within months, the publisher recalled the book, Lehrer was publicly disgraced, and he had to resign from his job as staff writer at *The New Yorker*.

Why? Because he'd violated the rules of nonfiction writing by making up a number of things that he said had come from sources, including some Bob Dylan quotations. He was busted by Michael C. Moynihan, a reporter and Dylan fan, who contacted Lehrer about the source of the quotations. After trying to evade the questions, Lehrer eventually admitted, "The quotes in question either did not exist, were unintentional misquotations, or represented improper combinations of previously existing quotes" (qtd. in Kearney).

Lehrer hurt not only himself with his misuse of sources; public trust in long-form journalism and other nonfiction genres decreases every time a scandal like this one surfaces.

In some instances, the mishandling of source material can have even more serious repercussions. As Daniel Engber reports in "Bad Footnotes Can Be Deadly," indiscriminant reliance on a single source has contributed to the opioid addiction epidemic in North America. In 1980, Jane Porter and Hershel Jick, medical researchers who studied whether prescribing narcotics[2] for hospitalized patients led to dependency, published a 101-word note in the *New England Journal of Medicine*, concluding that "despite widespread use of narcotic drugs in hospitals, the development of addiction is rare in medical patients with no history of addiction." In the next three decades, this note was cited hundreds of times in medical research articles to "support the claim that prescription painkillers weren't that addictive," leading to an increase in prescriptions (Engber).

Of course, we now know that these drugs are very addictive; the evidence is all around us. So what went wrong? It's likely that many who cited Porter and Jick were re-citing from the succeeding research articles instead of going back the original text. If they had read the original source, they would have noticed several crucial details:

- The Porter and Jick publication was only a note, not a research article, and therefore it hadn't gone through the peer-review process (which we describe at length in Chapter Two).
- The note contains little information about the methodologies used or how addiction was defined (it's only 101 words, after all).
- Porter and Jick studied only hospitalized patients; they did not investigate how patients respond to these drugs when they're prescribed outside of a hospital setting.

As the preceding examples show, lack of knowledge about how to evaluate and use sources effectively has a number of negative consequences, ranging from the embarrassing to the deadly.

That's why all of this matters and why we wrote this book.

---

2 Opioids are a subclass of narcotics.

What You'll Learn from *Who's Your Source?*

We titled this book *Who's Your Source?* for a reason. We want to encourage you to think about the person or persons behind every text that you encounter, that is, the authors whose works you read and reference in your own writing. Just like us, those authors are human beings prone to their own subjective views of the world.

Does this mean that all sources are equally unreliable? No. However, to distinguish between reliable and unreliable sources, we need to be discerning readers and researchers. This book aims to teach you how to become such a reader/researcher.

After reading this book, you will be equipped with the knowledge and skills you need to evaluate sources and the confidence to use them well in your writing.

In Chapter One, we introduce you to the Three Rs, our three-part strategy for evaluating sources. Based on rhetorical principles, the Three Rs present you with a framework that you'll find useful for any writing assignment that requires you to use sources.

Chapter Two covers academic sources, from journal articles to disciplinary encyclopedias. You'll learn the differences between academic genres and gain an understanding of the peer-review process. This is the longest chapter in *Who's Your Source?* because we recognize that most of the writing you do as a student will require you to incorporate material from academic sources.

There will be times, however, when you want to cite non-academic sources. Thus, Chapter Three discusses situations in which this would be appropriate and teaches you how to tell the difference between reliable and unreliable non-academic sources, including texts from newspapers, magazines, social media, websites, and *Wikipedia*. We also cover the phenomenon of fake news in this chapter, providing you with tips for differentiating the real from the fake.

Chapter Four describes common argumentative mishaps—logical fallacies—and includes illustrative examples to help you avoid faulty reasoning in your writing and recognize it in other people's arguments.

Before you can evaluate sources, though, you need to find them. Many of the students that we've worked with over the years have an incomplete understanding of how to conduct an efficient search and how much time they should reserve to find the right sources. In Chapter Five, The Search, we guide you through this process.

Chapter Six introduces you to methods of research that professional and academic writers employ when they want to use people, instead of texts, as their sources. You will learn the value of gathering information through interviews, focus groups, and surveys, and how to use these methods effectively for your own research.

Visual rhetoric, the idea that visuals, like words, have a persuasive impact on audiences, is the subject of Chapter Seven. In this chapter, we show you how to evaluate sources such as graphs, tables, photographs, and videos, and how to use them appropriately.

In Chapter Eight, we show you how to approach writing like a pro, including instruction on how to use a research question to guide your source search and how to use sources dynamically to develop your argument.

The final chapter covers the mechanics of incorporating source materials into your work. You'll learn to differentiate between paraphrase and summary, avoid plagiarism, integrate an author's words into your own sentences, cite correctly, and more.[3]

We've asked several scienticians, and they agree that this book is much more useful than a course at Bovine University. We hope you enjoy it.

> A companion website for students includes exercises, additional sample student papers, and links to resources discussed in the book. Please visit at https://sites.broadviewpress.com/source/

---

3   In this book, we follow the style guidelines of the Modern Language Association (MLA) because this is the accepted style of our discipline. Your instructor might ask you to use another style guide, such as APA (American Psychological Association) or Chicago Manual of Style depending on the subject of the course. We don't offer detailed style guidelines in this book, but you can find many online. We recommend the Purdue OWL (Online Writing Lab).

CHAPTER ONE

The Other Three Rs
A Three-Part Evaluation Strategy

A. Introduction to Rhetoric

Rhetoric is the art of attempting to inform and persuade a specific audience. *Rhetorical analysis* is what we do when we analyze how (and to what effect) an arguer makes her argument. Rhetoric is important because we use it to produce and analyze discourse. In other words, knowledge of rhetoric can help us write more convincingly; it can also help us understand the ways we are persuaded or even manipulated by the discourse we read, hear, and see.

Vocabulary note
Discourse refers to any written or spoken form of communication.

The fundamental point here is that everything you read, write, and say is the product of rhetorical choices (some more conscious than others).

Take the simple task of asking a teacher a question. You need to do so in a rhetorically sound way, which means considering the following questions:

- What should my tone be?
- When should I ask?
- Should I ask in person, or can I do so over email?
- How should I address the teacher?
- Do I need to give any background information or context?
- What words will most clearly pose the question?
- What should I avoid so I don't come off as needy, rude, or dumb?

Even when you're not persuading, you're using rhetoric. Suppose you want to simply explain to someone how to get to the financial aid office—you will still make rhetorical choices in doing so.

This chapter will take you through rhetorical terms and show you how to do rhetorical analysis.

What Are the Three Rs?

You have likely seen three Rs referenced in a number of different contexts. There are the three Rs of waste reduction (reduce, reuse, and recycle); the three Rs of ethical animal research (replacement, reduction, and refinement); the three Rs of Keynesian economics (relief, recovery, and reform); and the three Rs of education (reading, writing, and arithmetic), which may confuse primary school students since two of those items clearly don't begin with R!

THE OTHER THREE Rs   25

While all of those Rs are important, we'd like you to put those aside for the moment and consider the other three Rs: Rhetorical Appeals, Rhetorical Situation, and Reality Check. These three Rs comprise our three-part strategy for evaluating the ethics and effectiveness of any source you may encounter.

While no source evaluation strategy is 100 per cent foolproof, the Three Rs strategy presents you with tools that have worked for a large number of students we have taught in a broad range of university-level courses. You will be able to apply this strategy for assignments in any course that requires you to locate and incorporate reliable sources into your own writing. You'll likewise be able to apply this strategy to tasks that you will encounter when you graduate and enter the professional world. Beyond the realms of school and work, the Three Rs will also serve you well as a world citizen who wishes to assess the trustworthiness of the multiple sources of information we encounter daily.

B. Rhetorical Appeals: Logos, Ethos, Pathos

Some say the first university was established c. 900 CE, but 1200 years before that, Aristotle was talking about the three ways an arguer must appeal to her audience to have a great argument: logos, ethos, and pathos.

Logos: Logic
This, obviously, should be the basis of an argument. Arguers should have a logical main argument and then argue it with logical reasoning and evidence.

Check out the ways the authors you're reading establish logos:

- Organizing clearly
- Using facts, including anecdotes, studies, statistics, quotes from credible authors
- Using reasoning, deductive/inductive, etc.

- Avoiding logical fallacies (which we discuss at length in Chapter Four)
- Qualifying their arguments

An example of logos would be the factual, logical reason why many places have needle exchange programs, which allow drug addicts access to clean needles. While some make emotion-based claims that drug addicts don't deserve help or that needle exchanges might encourage drug use, the evidence is clear. Many rigorous scientific studies have shown that needle exchange programs significantly decrease diseases like HIV and hepatitis, while not encouraging further drug use. In fact, some studies have shown that needle exchange programs are correlated with more people seeking drug treatment (since the places that house needle exchanges have services for people wanting to quit). A lawmaker who won't support such programs usually cites an emotional reason for doing so, but logos, or logic, leads us to support these programs (if the goal is a healthier population).

John Oliver, on his show, *Last Week Tonight*, made a similar argument about spending money to prevent lead poisoning in children in America ("Episode 68"). All 50 US states have some areas with problematic lead pipes and lead paint in houses. Oliver cited a study that concluded, "Each dollar invested in lead paint hazard control results in a return of $17–221 [for the state]." Oliver is clearly showing it is logical to invest in this type of program, but he notes that this logical reason is "a distant third on [his] list of reasons not to poison children." Here, he is saying the emotional reason to help children is good enough for him, but he gives a logical reason for members of the audience who might not share his values.

One of the easiest ways to demonstrate a lack of logos is to make a ridiculous claim. Often, these are unqualified, meaning the author implies that the argument applies to everyone.

Here are some actual arguments we've seen in student essays:

No one wears watches anymore.
No one carries cash anymore.
Everyone has a smart phone.

Ummm...no.

The students here need to use qualifiers, words that make the meaning more specific by intensifying or clarifying it. One could argue that *fewer people* today wear watches and carry cash and go without smart phones. Be careful, though, some qualifiers could make your claim inaccurate: "Before cell phones, the *only* way people could talk to each other was writing letters." Before cell phones, there were *phones* (and other ways to communicate besides letters).

Think through word choice: is someone saying *proves*, when she means *implies* or *suggests*?

Maybe an author has a very logical argument. He sees a problem. He lays out a solution that he believes will be effective and time/cost efficient. Is he done?

No—he also has to make sure to appeal to ethos and pathos.

Ethos: Credibility

Warning: this is sometimes mistranslated as "ethics." Arguing that action x is ethical isn't about ethos (that's actually pathos—or an emotion-based claim). However, ethics still applies here; we have to be *ethical arguers* to establish credibility. An ethical arguer argues fairly, uses logos effectively, attempts to avoid bias (one can have a point of view without being biased), and shows that she has sufficient knowledge to make the argument.

Let's think about sufficient knowledge first. Is the author enough of an expert on the subject to talk about it? Say an author wants to fix a problem. Does he know why it became a problem (why it got set up that way)? Has he looked at *all* the possible solutions—why they would work, how they would work, what the effects of implementing them would be?

In other words, has he done his research?

If we see a problem with the way a course is designed, for example, before we talk about changing it, we need to figure out why it was set up that way in the first place. Did the department need a course that could satisfy more students? Was there a campus initiative this course was designed to fulfill? Let's say the course was originally created because the Dean's office wanted our department to have a large lecture class several years ago. The class just isn't working well. If we're going to change it, we will need to show the Dean that we now have other large lecture classes. Only then can we propose the change.

Without that knowledge, we would be arguing to our Dean without sharing the Dean's assumptions about how course sizes fulfill students' needs, and we thus wouldn't be addressing her concerns.

There are other ways to have sufficient knowledge, of course. One might have experience with the issue. If one has worked in sales, and the argument is about sales, the author usually mentions these credentials. Someone wanting to learn about childbirth could read books and articles, talk to an obstetrician, and talk to women who've had children. Each method is about a different aspect of ethos: the researcher is trying to find a credible, trustworthy source.

Can You Have Too Much Ethos?

We have to note one odd reality about ethos. Sometimes, people will associate experience with bias. This is most easily seen with politicians. Being a "career" politician—in other words, having experience—is seen as a negative, while we are trusted *more* as teachers because it's our career. Some dismiss whole groups of people with experience; this is usually when privilege is being challenged. For example, we are women and have experienced sexism and sexual harassment. Some people might dismiss our experience because they would consider us unreliable experts on our own lives. When our male colleagues defend feminism and challenge sexism and its abuses, however, people listen. As they are not victims of these particular systemic problems, they somehow are granted a higher level of credibility when discussing it.

Similarly, black people in the Jim Crow South were well aware of the racism around them, but were dismissed (the Jim Crow South refers to a time after black Americans were freed from slavery, but were still subject to incredibly racist laws and to segregation). It can't possibly be that bad, white people said. Then, in 1961, John Howard Griffin, a white journalist from the North, published a book: *Black Like Me*. Griffin had artificially altered the color of his skin and gone to the South, where he was perceived as a black man. The book was a bestseller: it was believable. In other words, the experiences of a white man who was "black" for a little while were deemed more trustworthy than the experiences of people who had been black their whole lives.

We need to be aware of a tendency to dismiss people's experiences, especially when those experiences run counter to how we see the world. We shouldn't think that people have "too much ethos."

Publishers highlight their authors' ethos. Why else would they tell us anything about the author or show us a picture of him? *The New Yorker*, for example, puts the following statement below articles by Atul Gawande: "Atul Gawande, a surgeon and public-health researcher, became a New Yorker staff writer in 1998." When we go to his author profile on the website, we get even more information:

Atul Gawande has been a staff writer for *The New Yorker* since 1998. He is the author of three best-selling books: "Complications," a finalist for the National Book Award; "Better," selected by Amazon.com as one of the 10 best books of 2007; and "The Checklist Manifesto." His latest book is

"Being Mortal: Medicine and What Matters in the End." He
has won the Lewis Thomas Prize for Writing about Science, a
MacArthur fellowship, and two National Magazine Awards.
He is also a surgeon at Brigham and Women's Hospital, in
Boston, and a professor in the department of health policy
and management at Harvard School of Public Health and in
the department of surgery at Harvard Medical School. He
is the executive director of Ariadne Labs, a joint center for
health-systems innovation, and the chairperson of Lifebox,
a nonprofit organization making surgery safer globally.

Gawande writes about health and medicine, and he's a doctor; we
are being told that he's an expert in his field and, therefore, that
we can trust him.

Gawande situates himself into most of his pieces; in other words,
he uses "I." For example, he starts an article entitled "Overkill"
with "it was lunchtime before my afternoon surgery clinic, which
meant that I was at my desk, eating a ham-and-cheese sandwich
and clicking through medical articles." The story both catches
our attention—what did he see in those articles?—and reminds
us that he's an expert, one who tries to keep up with innovations
in his field.

Gawande reports that he read an article about doctors ordering
too much care—too many expensive and unhelpful tests. He decides
to investigate: "In my clinic that afternoon, I saw eight new patients
with records complete enough that I could review their past medical history in detail.... To my surprise, it appeared that seven of
those eight had received unnecessary care." This particular use
of ethos is remarkably effective. Not only are we reminded of his
credentials, but his attention; he checks what he reads, just as you
should. He also admits that he doesn't know everything. A doctor
reading this piece may initially reject the idea that there's even
such a thing as too much care, as Gawande did. When Gawande,
a master of his field, admits he learned something new, the doctor
can feel more open to learning too.

We should note that all of Gawande's articles have added ethos because they're published in *The New Yorker*, a highly respected magazine featuring excellent long-form journalism.

Another way we build ethos is to borrow other people's. That's why we cite sources and why we set them up when we introduce them. We're saying, "We aren't the expert, but we learned from one!" For example, Michael Pollan goes to great lengths to explain why he uses Temple Grandin's words and ideas about what will happen to a steer going through a slaughterhouse, for his article "Power Steer":

> What I know about what happens on the far side of the blue door comes mostly from Temple Grandin, who has been on the other side and, in fact, helped to design it. Grandin, an assistant professor of animal science at Colorado State, is one of the most influential people in the United States cattle industry. She has devoted herself to making cattle slaughter less stressful and therefore more humane by designing an ingenious series of cattle restraints, chutes, ramps and stunning systems. Grandin is autistic, a condition she says has allowed her to see the world from the cow's point of view. The industry has embraced Grandin's work because animals under stress are not only more difficult to handle but also less valuable: panicked cows produce a surge of adrenaline that turns their meat dark and unappetizing. "Dark cutters," as they're called, sell at a deep discount.
>
> Grandin designed the double-rail conveyor system in use at the National Beef plant; she has also audited the plant's killing process for McDonald's. Stories about cattle "waking up" after stunning only to be skinned alive prompted McDonald's to audit its suppliers in a program that is credited with substantial improvements since its inception in 1999. Grandin says that in cattle slaughter "there is the pre-McDonald's era and the post-McDonald's era—it's night and day."

Grandin recently described to me what will happen to No. 534 [the steer Pollan bought as he was researching the article] after he passes through the blue door. "The animal goes into the chute single file," she began....

This technique works because Grandin is indeed an expert. Your sources should use good sources themselves, sources with the requisite knowledge, sources without bias, etc. In other words, if you're reading a scientific article about the health effects of sugar, that source should be backing up its claims with evidence from its own studies and with information from other scientists, not from members of congress with no scientific training (but whose district has a booming sugar industry) or from members of the sugar industry with an interest in denying or downplaying sugar's negative effects. However, the article may cite those sources when discussing public health knowledge or the problems in implementing public health safety measures.

An ethical arguer will be fair. In other words, she will acknowledge other viewpoints, representing them accurately. If her side is "right" and she has the evidence to back it up, she doesn't need to slander the other side, ignore it, or even oversimplify. She can simply say, "Some are against this measure because of the initial high cost, but we'll be making that money back after just three years." She won't say, "Some stupid people..." or "some people who don't want us to succeed..."[1] That would be biased and immature. If you see arguments like that, ask yourself: why isn't this person showing respect to the points of view of others? Is this person actually arguing logically or just trying to get me to fear the other side?

We also need to be aware of our own biases when evaluating sources. For example, in the 2016 US Presidential election, independent agencies like PolitiFact rated Hillary Clinton as one of the most truthful politicians in America. However, she was called

---

1 This is an example of a straw man logical fallacy, which we'll discuss in Chapter Four.

a liar so often (she was nicknamed "lying Hillary" and "crooked Hillary" by her opponents) that many people would just assume she was lying about any given thing, and, due to their own biases, would not check the information with a reliable source.

Did you just have a knee-jerk reaction to that example? Did you say, "No way! She's a liar!!!" OR "of course! I knew she never lies"? Our example was factual, but if you had either response and didn't think to check for yourself, then you just fell victim to the kind of bias to which we're all prone.

A long time ago, on an episode of *The Simpsons*, Marge Simpson was watching President Bill Clinton talk about an upcoming election—she didn't know his body was inhabited by an alien, Kodos.

Kodos: I am Clin-Ton. As overlord, all will kneel trembling before me and obey my brutal commands. End communication.
Marge: Hmm, that's Slick Willie for you, always with the smooth talk.
("Treehouse of Horror VII")

Marge clearly shared a common belief about Bill Clinton, that he was a smooth talker. It altered her ability to actually hear what he said.

As we encounter other people's arguments, we need to evaluate them and ourselves for "confirmation bias." This is when we only see facts that correspond to a point of view we already have. Ethical arguers and ethical researchers understand this bias and try to fight it. We'll discuss confirmation bias at greater length in the Reality Check section of this chapter.

The bottom line: If an argument is logical, but the author seems untrustworthy or not knowledgeable, the argument will not succeed.

Evaluate your sources for ethos:

- Where does the author establish his credibility?
- Where does the author establish the credibility of his sources?

- Where does the author establish that he's fair—is he engaging with counter-argument well?
- Is the work published in a reputable source?

Red flags:

- The source has no author.
- The source has no clear publication or update date.
- There's no way to contact the author or webmaster to ask questions.
- The author doesn't seem to know what he's talking about.
- The author is clearly biased.
- The author is making claims without any evidence or sources to back him up.
- The author is engaging in logical fallacies to trick you or to make the other side look silly (see Chapter Four).
- The piece is published in a less than reputable source.
- The piece is posing as news, but is actually opinion or editorial.
- The piece was published on a satire site (like *The Onion* or *The Beaverton*).
- The piece overly relies on ethos—that is, there is no logic—the author is just saying, "trust me; I know."

Counter-argument

Note that many of the questions in this chapter might lead us to consider another aspect of a rhetorical argument—when an author responds to possible questions or objections a reader might have.

One of Karma's students recently addressed a counter-argument immediately after stating her thesis, which was about how Shakespeare portrays Shylock and Edgar in their respective plays: "It is important to note that this essay is not claiming that these villains are completely innocent but examining the various ways Shakespeare depicts these characters sympathetically." The student was savvy enough to realize that her audience may misunderstand a goal of the paper. The best way to avoid misunderstandings is to be explicit with your audience about what you're doing.

Often, though, counter-argument needs more attention than just one sentence.

One of our friends, Courtney, lives in the UK. She was reading a blog by an American writer she admires about the importance of vaccinating children. Courtney noticed that the author spent a lot of time addressing the concerns of anti-vaxxers, which led her to realize that meant many Americans *were* anti-vaxxers. A British blog wouldn't necessarily respectfully engage anti-vaxxers, as it's not a common position in that country. In fact, it might not mention the "cons" to vaccination at all, since the British public largely doesn't think there are any.

In other words, the fact that an American author had to engage with a particular counter-argument taught Courtney about American audiences and the context of the vaccine discussion in America.

The context and the audience will change how an author deals with counter-argument. If we're writing about vaccines to healthcare professionals, we won't spend time debunking anti-vaccine myths. If we want to persuade parents who are worried about vaccines not to be, then we *must* engage with their concerns, and we must do so in a way that will be persuasive *to them*.

An ethical arguer will engage with counter-argument fairly and respectfully, conceding and refuting as she goes. That is, she will concede some of the points (she would acknowledge, for example, that there are very rare occasions when vaccines do cause harm; she would refute this objection with statistics about the much higher number of children who are hurt by lack of vaccination).

Note, though, that if the "other side" is ridiculous, you don't need to address it. Nor do you have to give counter-arguments "equal time" in your arguments. A student writing about the medical experiments conducted during the Holocaust in WWII doesn't need to address the crazy (racist) minority that claims the Holocaust never happened. If 99 per cent of studies have similar conclusions, the 1 per cent shouldn't get 50 per cent of the attention.

Engaging with counter-argument is one of the ways we tackle the underlying *assumptions* we're making about our audience. The underlying assumptions we make while we argue are called *warrants*. Most of our assumptions concerning our audience are about what we're assuming they already *know* and what they already *believe*. For example, if we make the argument that something should be outlawed because it's a mortal sin, we are assuming our audience believes in sin, that they believe in the classification of sins that would make some of them "mortal," that they know what a mortal sin is, and that they believe in legislating morality. If our audience disagrees with any of these assumptions, the argument will fail before it even gets started. If our audience agrees with these assumptions, they probably won't even notice that we're making them.

Every argument has warrants. At the most basic level, *each word* is an acknowledgement of an assumption. If we use a word, but don't define it, we're assuming our audience knows it. If we use a word and stop to define it, we're assuming they don't know it yet. Note how we can get in trouble easily if our assumptions are wrong.

Authors do not explicitly address warrants. That is, an author won't say, "I'm writing this in English because I assume that's what you read" or "I'm defining this word because I assume you may be unfamiliar with it." Warrants exist *underneath* the surface argument; they are taken for granted by the author.

As you analyze other people's arguments (and your own), ask yourself these questions about counter-argument and assumptions:

- Does the author engage with counter-argument?
- Where does the author engage with it?
- Does the author address all possible questions or problems the audience might have?
- Is the author respectful of opposition points?
- Is the author fair, and does he concede when he needs to?
- Does he convincingly refute the counter-points?
- If he doesn't engage with particular issues or points of view, why might he be ignoring or avoiding them?

Pro-Tip!

Many students were taught in secondary school that the counter-argument should come at the end of a paper, before the conclusion. This is the weakest place to put a counter-argument. Think about it: you've made your point, but then you bring up all the reasons you could be wrong, all the exceptions...you had better be able to refute perfectly before that conclusion. Try doing counter-argument as you go along (mention the exception, and point out that it's just an exception, in paragraph two, when you're already talking about that issue) or at the beginning of the essay—that way, you'll have your whole essay to refute!

Pathos: Emotional Appeal

Let's say someone is asking us to donate money to a charity. We agree that there is a need and that this money will help alleviate the problem (logos). We think the charity is trustworthy (ethos).

Will we donate the money?

Not unless the issue touches our emotions, too. That's why we need pathos.

At the most basic level, you need someone to care enough about your argument to keep reading it. If you want them to take action— to vote a certain way, to sign a petition, to change how they operate customer service—you have to get them to care a lot.

Evaluating pathos:

- Where does the author share a story?
- Where does the author talk about consequences of taking/not taking an action?
- What emotions is the author appealing to, directly and through implication (lust, fear, etc.)?
- Where does the author try to make the audience *care*?

The easiest places to see pathos at work are commercials. If we associate a sports star you love with our pillows, you'll be more likely to buy them. Michelin has a series of ads with the slogan "a lot is riding on your tires"; one ad shows a car driving on a dark and rainy night. The infant of the driver is in the back seat: that's what's riding on your tires. Michelin wants you to fear what might happen to those you love if your tires are subpar.

Most every beer ad in the world is famous for associating drinking with sex, hoping that your lust will translate into sales. Don't even get us started on the body spray ones.

Some students overlook one of the most valuable emotions to appeal to: a sense of humor. We are more likely to sit through a commercial that's funny and more likely to associate positive feelings to the product that's now associated with making us smile. That's why so many arguers choose to use humor. For example, people might not want to read a long, formal essay on the problems of plastic pollution; they would much rather watch *The Majestic Plastic Bag*, a satirical nature documentary about a plastic bag's journey to the Pacific Ocean (see also Chapter Seven).

You might be thinking: politicians appeal to pathos a lot too. Bingo!

Politicians and marketers (and those who market politicians) know that the myth of the rational actor is just that: a myth. Economic theory used to rely on the idea that people make rational choices when they have the right information. A few decades ago, social scientists proved that false. Humans respond to emotion, often letting it over-ride rationality.

In fact, if someone is very opposed to a position, hearing more facts actually causes the person to dig into their original belief more. A recent article summed up many studies about it this way: "Don't just keep explaining why climate change is real—explain how climate change will hurt public health or the local economy. Communication that appeals to values, not just intellect, research shows, can be far more effective" (Requarth). This is especially important when the belief is part of a person's *identity*. Someone might not mind being wrong about which star was in what movie, but a person who doesn't believe in climate change often has that belief tied to a political identity.

In other words, when we want to convince someone, doing so through pathos can be even more effective than logos.

Many arguers resist using pathos as they see it as a form of manipulation, but all persuasion has some elements of manipulation. This is why ethos is so important. To use pathos effectively, arguers must be ethical; they must be fair.

Moreover, just as an argument is flawed if it relies too heavily on ethos, it's flawed if it relies too heavily on pathos. The argument still needs facts and logic at its center.

Think of this like a pie. A pie needs a solid bottom to hold it together: this is the ethos. The whipped or iced cream or meringue topping is very pretty: it's the pathos. The actual pie is the logic, and it should be the majority of an argument.

When you see someone throw a pie into someone else's face in comedy, you're only seeing someone throw a pie pan filled with whipped cream.

If you want to eat that pie, you need the actual pie in there. It's not a pie without it.

Be wary of sources that are all pie pan or all whipped cream.

Be aware of your own position as you evaluate. If you don't find an argument convincing, is it because the logic doesn't hold up? Because you think the author is biased? Because it doesn't appeal to your values? Because you simply don't care about that subject?

Pro-Tip!

A savvy arguer will also attempt to persuade an audience through pathos that targets the audience's core values, rather than the arguer's. For example, think back to John Oliver making an argument about fixing lead water pipes in America. He knew that his values (morality) wouldn't persuade everyone. He needed to appeal to a different emotion, greed, and thus he made a logical appeal about saving money. The politician trying to justify a needle exchange program should appeal to logic, of course, but the politician also needs to appeal to those who make these judgments based on emotions. In that case, the politician needs to explain that this program is logical and moral.

Karma recently needed to persuade her landlord to replace an old, ineffective dishwasher. While she explained that it didn't work well, she particularly stressed how much more water she was using, running more cycles to get the dishes clean and empty cycles to try to clean the mineral deposits out. Although the landlord may not care about the cleanliness of her dishes, he cares about the water bill: because he pays it. She now has a new dishwasher.

Telos and Kairos

Logos, ethos, and pathos are the three most common appeals, but Aristotle talked about two more. Telos is the purpose of an argument. If you go to a seminar to learn about various ways to solve a problem, only to discover that the speaker is trying to persuade you to buy their product, you will be upset; the speaker's telos is different from yours.

Kairos refers to the setting: when and where does this argument appear? Setting will of course affect how an argument is presented and how it is received. Imagine the difference between arguing for universal background checks for firearm sales to an audience of National Rifle Association members versus Parent Teacher Association members. Imagine reading an argument for equal pay for women in *The Economist* versus reading one in *Maxim*. Imagine reading that argument in an essay from 1910, from 1960, and from 2010.

These ideas are expanded upon in the next section.

C. Rhetorical Situation: Genre, Audience, Purpose, Context

Scholars and instructors in the field of Writing Studies use the term rhetorical situation to refer to the set of circumstances in which a text appears. All texts have a rhetorical situation, even those that were not produced for an *evidently* persuasive purpose. (We use the word "evidently" here because we hope that by the time you have finished reading this book, we will have persuaded you that *all* texts have a persuasive purpose—even that lab report you have to turn in on Tuesday morning.) Like rhetorical appeals, the elements of rhetorical situation are universally applicable to your evaluation of any text.

In the following sections, we introduce you to each element of rhetorical situation: genre, audience, purpose, and context.

Genre

You may have learned about genre (which simply means type or category) when taking a literature course. In Literary Studies, genre refers to categories such as poetry, drama, creative nonfiction, and fiction. Within each category, there may also be sub-genres; fiction sub-genres include science fiction, detective novels, romance novels, and fantasy.

In Writing Studies, the concept of genre is applied to all texts, literary or not. As a student, you have been asked to write a number of academic genres, including argumentative essays, research papers, and lab reports. If you go on to graduate school, you will be required to compose other academic genres: dissertations, annotated bibliographies, grant proposals, research articles, and conference abstracts. Beyond academia, there are workplace genres, such as resumes, cover letters, memos, and press releases, as well as everyday genres like email correspondence, social network posts, and newspaper editorials.

So beyond knowing that the term "genre" applies to *all* texts, what's the point?

The point is that every genre has its own conventions. Genre conventions are the features readers expect to see or the moves they expect a writer to make in any given text. Teachers, editors, reviewers, and others make judgments about the effectiveness of a text based on how well it adheres to the conventions of the genre. You, too, will need to learn how to evaluate a text in light of genre conventions. These may include structure, word choice, length, and citation practices.

Let's take, for example, the scientific research article.

Most peer-reviewed science journals will only publish research articles that are structured in IMRaD format. IMRaD stands for Introduction, Methods, Results, and Discussion.[2] A group of scientists may have come up with extraordinary results in their most recent study, but if they lump the methods and results sections together in their article, it's unlikely to be approved by reviewers or reach its intended audience of other members of the scientific community.

Word choice and style are also considerations. Writers of research articles tend to use highly technical terms without defining them because they assume that their intended audience of other experts in the same field will already be familiar with the vocabulary. For example, an article recently published in *The Canadian Journal of Anesthesia/Journal canadien d'anesthésie* is titled "Optimal Dose of Intrathecal Isobaric Bupivacaine in Total Knee Arthroplasty" (van Egmond et al.). Nowhere in the article do the authors define isobaric bupivacaine. Doing so would likely lead the intended audience of other researchers to feel impatient, or worse, indignant at the writers' condescension.

Throughout this article, you will encounter many sentences written in the passive voice, such as the following: "The dose was increased or decreased by steps of 0.5 mg, depending on the outcome of the preceding patient" (van Egmond et al. 1004). Revised for active voice, the sentence would look like this: "We increased or

---

2   See Chapter Two for an explanation of IMRaD format and its relationship to scientific research.

decreased the dose by steps of 0.5 mg, depending on the outcome of the preceding patient." An English teacher may have told you that you should avoid using the passive voice in your writing. Applying this advice to this article might lead you to conclude that this is an example of bad writing. This conclusion, however, disregards the genre conventions of the scientific research article, which allows for the use of passive voice as a method that research writers may employ to avoid referring to themselves ("I" or "we") directly in their articles.[3]

Genre conventions also have some bearing on the rhetorical appeals that are or aren't emphasized in a given text. Research articles tend to rely heavily on ethos and logos, while de-emphasizing pathos, which might be more appropriate for different genres and audiences. At the end of the article in the *Canadian Journal of Anesthesia*, you will find a lengthy reference list of the resources that the writers cited throughout. Long reference lists are common in research articles. It is one of the ways that research writers demonstrate their own credibility (or ethos).

Does this mean that you should automatically judge a source as lacking credibility if no citations are included? No. Citations are not expected for some genres. We have seen too many students question the credibility of newspaper and magazine writers because they haven't incorporated citations into their texts. However, when was the last time you read a newspaper article that had a reference list? It's just not part of the genre conventions for the newspapers or general audience magazines.

Understanding genre is an important aspect of evaluating the effectiveness of a text. You must ask yourself:

- What genre is this?
- What are the conventions of this genre?
- How well does this particular text fulfill those conventions?

---

3 Note, however, that even in a scientific article, most sentences are written in the active voice.

You may find it difficult to answer some of these questions if you're reading a genre that is new to you. If that's the case, you need to do a little bit of homework, which might include reading other examples of the genre or asking your instructor for some tips on the conventions.

Audience

In our preceding discussion of genre, we referred to audience as well. This is because the intended audience for any text is intimately related to genre. In fact, all four aspects of rhetorical situation are necessarily related to one another, and you must consider them in conjunction with one another when evaluating a source.

You have likely put some thought into your intended audience when writing for your classes. Think about the last time you were drafting a paper for a class assignment. You might have asked yourself some of the following questions:

- How will my instructor and classmates react to what I'm writing?
- Am I including enough reliable evidence to convince my instructor and classmates that my interpretation or argument is valid?
- Am I sufficiently demonstrating my knowledge on this subject?
- Am I using language appropriate for this assignment?
- Do I need to define some of my terms?
- Have I met all of the instructor's requirements for this assignment?

In asking these questions, you were envisioning your instructor and potentially your classmates as your intended audience. You were considering how to meet the needs of your intended audience and how to appeal to that audience through ethos, pathos, and logos.

Successful published writers ask themselves versions of the same questions about their intended audiences. Thus, you can redirect the questions above when you evaluate sources for how effectively they address the needs of the intended audience. Before you begin, however, you need to make sure you understand whom the intended audience is. Unless you are already a medical professional, you are not the intended audience for the *Canadian Journal of Anesthesia* article that we used as an example in the previous section. It would be wrong to assume that the authors of that article were not meeting the needs of the audience because they haven't defined isobaric bupivacaine. On the other hand, a writer reporting on this same study for a so-called general audience magazine, such as *Discover*, would be lax if she didn't offer her audience a definition.

Did you notice how we just qualified the general audience as "so-called"? That's because we don't really believe in the general audience.

Sometimes writers, editors, and writing instructors use the term "general audience" when referring to any non-specialist audience. However, this is just a catchall term: there is no such thing as a completely general audience. No piece of writing is intended to meet the needs of all readers from the age of 6 to 106, without regard to education level or individual interests.

Just taking a glance through the *Writer's Market* (an annually published reference book that helps freelance writers find appropriate publications for their work) will give you a sense of just how varied supposedly "general" audiences may be. Take for instance the following descriptions for two different magazines that are listed in the "General Interest" section of the *Writer's Market 2018*:

> [*Family Circle* is] a national, general interest women's magazine that focuses on all subjects relating to the family.... Needs essays, opinion, personal experience, women's interest subjects such as family and personal relationships, children, physical and mental health, nutrition, and self improvement....

> *Smithsonian Magazine*'s mission is to inspire fascination with all the world has to offer by featuring unexpected and entertaining editorial that explores different lifestyles, cultures and peoples, the arts, the wonders of nature and technology. The

highly educated, innovative readers of *Smithsonian* share a unique desire to celebrate life, seek out the timely as well as timeless, the artistic as well as the academic, and the thought-provoking as well as the humorous.

Can you see how differently these two magazines are imagining their readers? There's nothing "general" about them at all.

There may be some overlap in the readership of these two magazines, say, a mother with a master's degree who is interested in child-rearing tips *and* in the most recent archeological finds. We happen to know quite a few readers about whom that is true. However, such a reader does not expect a single publication to address all of her interests, and a writer who wants to publish in either magazine won't succeed if she tries to write an article that would be appropriate for both. She needs to imagine her intended audience as fitting squarely within the terms laid out in these descriptions.

Overall, then, the intended audience is the group of readers writers have in mind when they're composing a text. Your nutrition instructor might assign as reading a research article from the *American Journal of Clinical Nutrition*. If you don't immediately understand everything in the article, you cannot claim that the authors are not meeting the needs of the audience; their intended audience was other nutrition researchers, not students in an undergraduate course. You might not have the prior knowledge that the authors are assuming, but their intended audience does. Likewise, your housemate, who has no interest in technology and who rolls his eyes every time you suggest that he read a "great article" in the new issue of *Wired*, is not the intended audience for this magazine.

To evaluate a text for how effectively it meets the needs of the intended audience, you should ask yourself the following:

- Who is the intended audience?
- What might the audience seek to gain from reading this text and how effectively is the text fulfilling those desires?

- What prior knowledge is the author assuming on the part of this audience? In other words, what warrants exist in the piece?
- How is the author using rhetorical appeals to engage this audience?
- How does the author use pronouns? Does she refer to herself as "I"? Is she including the audience when she writes "we"? Or does she not refer to herself at all in the text? Answering questions about pronoun use can give you a sense of how close or distant of a relationship the writer is trying to create with her audience. (Pronouns also signal tone. "You" is generally not used in formal writing, for example.)

Purpose (Telos)

The purposes of texts are as varied as their intended audiences. Some writers compose texts to persuade or inform, others to entertain their intended audiences. Moreover, some writers have multiple purposes in mind. For instance, our primary purpose in writing this is teaching you, our intended audience, how to evaluate and use sources effectively. We also hope to persuade you that our rhetorical framework offers the best approach to source evaluation and, occasionally, to entertain you a bit.

Misunderstanding the purpose of a text can lead to inappropriate evaluations. Take for example an article published in 2000 by *The Onion*. In "*Harry Potter* Books Spark Rise in Satanism among Children," *The Onion* writer quoted a number of children who had allegedly gone over to the dark side after reading J.K. Rowlings's popular children's books, including this from nine-year-old Ashley Daniels: "I used to believe in what they taught us in Sunday school.... But the Harry Potter books showed me that magic is real, something I can learn and use right now, and that the Bible is nothing but boring lies." The article led to hysteria among some US parents, who forbade their children to read the books (Benjamin).

There was, however, no real evidence suggesting a rise in Satan worshipping among *Harry Potter* readers. The hysteria arose simply because of a misunderstanding about the purpose of this text. *The Onion* is a satire newspaper. Its purpose is not to inform, but to entertain readers. Although *Onion* articles are in written in a journalistic style, they are not intended to be read as factual news articles. Ashley Daniels is as fictional as Harry Potter himself, and the quotation from her was pure make believe. The intended audience of *The Onion* understood this because they are familiar with the genre of satire and what they are seeking in its pages is nothing more than a few hearty laughs. We suspect that *The Onion* writers are also getting a few hearty laughs every time unintended audiences misunderstand their purpose, which happens more often than you might think. Chapter Three, on evaluating non-academic resources, will go over this in more detail.

Sometimes it is easy to figure out the purpose of a text. In an article published in *The Walrus*, Kelly Gallagher-Mackay and Nancy Steinhauer make their purpose clear in the title, "How Schools Can Stop Killing Creativity." They develop this purpose throughout the article by describing in detail several Canadian teachers' efforts to make space in their curriculum for their students' own creative projects. Similarly, newspaper reporters generally indicate their purpose in the lede (first sentence) of their articles. In many academic genres, writers announce their purpose in their thesis statements or preview it in an abstract. At other times, discovering the purpose of a text may require a bit more time and investigation.

Questions to consider with regard to purpose:

- What question or problem is the writer attempting to address in this text?
- What is the focus of the first one or two paragraphs?
- What is the context in which this text appears?

More on context follows in the next section.

There are several ways we classify the purpose of arguments.

The Purposes of Argument

- To inform (e.g., a website explaining California's Cash for Clunkers Program); yes, this is still an argument. The website writer is implicitly arguing that this is the proper way to do it.
- To explore (an in-depth analysis that doesn't necessarily take a side). These are *very* rare in published Western writing.
- To entertain (a joke).
- To persuade.

Types of Persuasion Arguments

- Arguments of Fact: Did something happen? Was the T-Rex primarily a predator or scavenger?
- Arguments of Definition: In this type of argument, you must define a term and then determine if your object fits the definition. Is ketchup a vegetable? Is this true love? Is Deadpool a hero, in the classical sense?
- Arguments of Evaluation: In this type of argument, you lay forth criteria and see if your argument fits it. Evaluation and definition are closely linked. Literary analysis usually falls into this category; the criteria include the literary criticism the author applies to the text. Compare and contrast arguments sometimes fall into this category, if the intention is to evaluate the strengths and weaknesses of the two items through the synthesis (if the intention is to propose a third option, then it's a proposal). Was Napoleon right to try to take Russia? Who's the best comedian in the country?
- Proposal Arguments: Argue for something to change or for action to be taken. For example, "Marriage should be for five years, with an option to renew."
- Causal Arguments: An argument about cause and effect. You can either see an effect and try to argue that it's the result of a certain cause, or you state a cause and then its effect: "Many students resist moving out of the five-paragraph format; this is

because high school teachers don't teach them anything else" or "the frequent use of emoji results in an inability to write formally."

We will expect you to be able to categorize arguments using these terms. Note that proper classification isn't about how much time the author spends doing a certain thing; it's about what the *overall* purpose is. For example, an author might spend 95 per cent of his time informing you about the dangers of human papillo-mavirus (HPV), but his goal would actually be to get you to be vaccinated, so his argument would be to persuade, to make a proposal. In this case, the *how* of the proposal is clear: schedule an appointment with a clinic or physician.

In many proposals, though, making the argument for *why* isn't enough. In the above proposal about marriage being for five years with an option to renew, the arguer would have to explain *how* this would work, after convincing someone that a change should be made: what government office would be in charge of tracking this? How much would it cost to renew? If there's a prenup, would that have to be renegotiated and renewed every time? If a couple didn't renew, are they automatically divorced or do they still have to go through a court proceeding?

Similarly, an arguer might spend a lot of that essay explaining the problems HPV causes, which might make you think it is a causal argument, but the goal isn't to persuade you that HPV leads to those complications, especially since the cause/effect isn't up for debate. Rather, he's informing you about the causes and effects in the service of his proposal.

As you analyze arguments, you should also be able to identify them in terms of time:

- Past (forensic) (an essay arguing that the dinosaurs were actually warm-blooded)
- Present (epideictic or ceremonial) (a politician arguing that America is #1 at a rally)

- Future (deliberative) (a NASA paper arguing for future space exploration)

Most arguments are deliberative: let's have Indian for lunch; here's how to find a better database for your research; etc.

Looking at the verb tense predominantly used in the essay is not the most accurate way to gauge time. The time period of the evidence does not always signal the time period of the argument. Instead, you want to think about purpose/thesis. Proposals are always deliberative. Evaluations are usually forensic or epideictic. (If the evaluation ends with you saying, "and, based on these criteria, we should do x," then of course you're actually in a proposal, though maybe not a persuasive one, since you haven't addressed *how*.)

Context (Kairos): Physical and Social

There are two aspects of context to consider: the physical and the social. Physical context refers to the actual space in which a text appears or is published. This might be a daily newspaper, like *The Globe and Mail*, an organizational website, such as that of the Southern Poverty Law Center, or a peer-reviewed academic journal. Understanding the physical context of a text is important because it provides us with clues in our quest to analyze the overall rhetorical situation and the rhetorical appeals employed.

Most newspapers and magazines are supported by advertising revenue, and readers will find ads for a variety of consumer products appearing alongside the articles they are reading, regardless of whether they are reading the print or online version of the publication. Advertising can have an impact on the content that appears in these contexts. For example, a cosmetic company may object to advertising its products in a woman's magazine that includes an article about going make-up free for the summer or that features women without make-up on the cover. In fact, some advertisers require magazines to create "complementary articles," those that suggest pink is in, for example. In contrast, when peer-reviewed journals include advertisements, they are usually for scholarly books or conferences that are relevant to the journal's specialized audience; typically, such advertisements are placed in the front or back matter of the journal, not alongside the articles themselves.

As an attentive reader, you must take into consideration the extent to which such advertising may or may not be a factor in the writer's credibility.

Taking a text out of its physical context can lead to gross misunderstandings of other aspects of the text's rhetorical situation. Indeed, this is one of the factors that led to the *Harry Potter* controversy we described earlier. Some readers who did not understand that *The Onion* is a satire magazine passed the article on via email (the fastest way to spread misinformation back in the pre-Facebook days) without mentioning where it had originally appeared.

Today, venues for spreading texts out of context have proliferated. Think of all the times you've seen texts re-posted on social networking sites. Maybe you've read some of these re-posted texts, responded to them, and even re-re-posted them yourself without considering the context in which they originally appeared. To be a savvy evaluator of texts, you need to make sure you understand the original, physical context (an issue that we will address at greater length in Chapters Two and Three).

Social context refers to the historical and cultural situation in which a text appears. For instance, many people today are aware of the problems that have arisen because of the over-prescription of antibiotics. You may know someone who has had an antibiotic resistant infection. The term "superbug" has entered into the general cultural conversation. This is the social context in which the article "How to Stop Overprescribing Antibiotics," which you'll read at the end of this chapter, appeared in the *New York Times Review* on 25 March 2016 (Fox, Linder, and Doctor). Because of the social context, the authors of this piece devoted only a few sentences to describing the problem and dedicated the rest of their article to offering a potential solution. They could safely assume that most of their readers were already aware of the problem.

When you are dealing with a text that originated in a social context other than your own, you need to consider the cultural and historical situation in which it originally appeared. For instance, Jonathan Swift's satirical essay, "A Modest Proposal," was first published in England in 1729. At the time, many of Swift's fellow Irishmen were impoverished and starving due to their treatment as colonized subjects of England. His "modest proposal" that the Irish should sell their babies as food for wealthy Englishmen cannot be understood without knowledge of this social context. Swift assumed that his intended audience would understand his purpose: to critique heartless English attitudes toward the problems in Ireland, problems largely caused by the English themselves.

Questions to ask about context:

- Where did this text originally appear?
- Who is the publisher or website sponsor?
- What is the publisher or website sponsor's purpose?
- Does this text appear in a site that also includes advertising?
- When was this text published and where (meaning geographical and publishing location)?
- What was the larger cultural conversation on this topic at the time of publication?

D. Reality Check

Recently, Melissa came upon the following statement in a book while she was conducting research for an article: "If you are an average American, forty years old, you're probably approaching banana 10,000" (Koeppel). What an incredible figure! Melissa is over forty and has always loved bananas, so she was amazed to learn that she may have eaten more than 10,000 bananas in her life so far.

The statement also seemed like just the thing Melissa needed to wow her intended audience, and the source seemed reliable. She knew that the author had published two award-winning books, including the one in which this statement was found. He'd been interviewed on a number of television and radio programs after publishing the book and had appeared as an expert in a documentary film about banana plantations in Central America. His book had also been praised by the Nobel Prize winning economist, Paul Krugman, as essential reading for understanding the flow of goods and capital in the global economy. Melissa incorporated the quotation into the introductory paragraph of her article, where she thought it would grab the reader's attention and also underscore one of the points she made in the body of the article: that the banana is America's favorite fruit.

However, when Melissa returned to her draft the next day and read the quotation again, she had the sense that the number was just too incredible to be true. Ten thousand bananas in 40 years? Really? That would be 250 bananas per person each year. She decided it was time for a Reality Check.

Melissa turned to the website of Statista, a market research organization that compiles data on consumer habits and other topics that are of interest to corporations, researchers, and educators. According to Statista, individual Americans consumed on average anywhere between 22 and 28.5 pounds of bananas each year between 2000 and 2016. Melissa felt that she could trust this information because Statista compiles data from over 22,000 different sources, their site is not supported by any advertising, and much of their content can only be accessed by subscribers. She had also seen similar banana consumption rates cited in a number of other sources that she'd read.

Melissa also learned through her investigation that the average banana weighs about 4 ounces, meaning that there are about four bananas in a pound. She did the math, and even when she was assuming a higher consumption rate per year, she found that the author's claim just didn't compute.

4 bananas x 28 pounds = 112 bananas per year
112 bananas x 40 years = 4,480 bananas

If the average American has consumed 10,000 bananas by the time of her 40th birthday, the pounds per year would have been closer to 60 pounds per year. Even though the data provided by Statista did not go back further than 2000, Melissa doubted the consumption rate could have been that much higher in the preceding years.

Fortunately, Melissa had decided to do the math on this claim before sending her final draft off to a publisher. She might have been drawing the wrong type of attention to her article by including that quotation in her introduction.

Though we hesitate to rely on platitudes in our teaching, in this the case the old adage holds true: if something seems too good (or astonishing or alarming or outrageous) to be true, it may be. As a researcher and writer, it is your job to step back from your sources and evaluate the plausibility of their claims. We call this Reality Check. Here are steps you can take to conduct a Reality Check on the sources you're reading.

Don't Jump to Conclusions

In 2014, a group of researchers in Finland conducted a study comparing the number of hours 4,000 Finnish men and women slept with the number of times they missed a day of work. The researchers concluded that women who get 7.6 hours of sleep per night and men who get 7.8 hours of sleep per night are the least likely to miss work (Lallukka et al.). Can we assume, based on this study, that getting close to eight hours of sleep will help us avoid illness? Not necessarily.

As James Hamblin, MD,[4] points out, statistics are tricky to interpret and apply. Eight hours is either "the amount of sleep that keeps people well, or that's the amount that makes them least likely to lie

---

4 Notice what we did here. We added MD after Hamblin's name to indicate the author we're quoting is a medical doctor and, therefore, he may be a trustworthy source of information on human health. In doing so, we are appealing to ethos. We are demonstrating our own credibility as writers by alluding to our source's credibility.

about being sick when they want to skip work. Or maybe people who were already sick with some chronic condition were sleeping more than that—or less—as a result of their illness" (Hamblin). Alternatively, as some of our students have pointed out, eight hours may be the amount of sleep Finnish people need to avoid sick days, but that isn't necessarily generalizable to other populations.

To be clear, we are not saying that the Finnish study is unreliable. The researchers who conducted this study used an effective methodology, and they are claiming only that, among their studied population, there is a *correlation* between the number of hours of sleep and the number of sick days. If you wanted to cite this study in a paper, you would need to avoid jumping to conclusions about what this study reveals about the relationship between sleep and health. Telling your readers about the limitations of your sources does not weaken your argument. In fact, doing so demonstrates your own credibility as a writer.

Play the Skeptic

Too often, we find that when students are given an assignment to write an argumentative essay, they begin to formulate a thesis statement before they have conducted any research. Their research agenda is then driven by the desire to find sources that support or agree with their thesis. In so doing, students often overlook or disregard other perspectives on their topics, which weakens rather than strengthens their arguments.

When we encounter discourse that agrees with our existing perspectives, we are susceptible to confirmation bias, which we mentioned earlier in the section on ethos. Confirmation bias can be defined as the tendency to believe statements or sources that confirm our own point of view. By the time Melissa read about banana 10,000, she had already learned from a number of other reliable sources that Americans eat more bananas than they do any other fruit, so she was inclined to believe her source. She was experiencing confirmation bias.

The trouble with confirmation bias is that it frequently leads us to stop questioning and to avoid looking for disconfirming sources or counterpoints. If you want to be an effective researcher and writer, as well as a responsible citizen, you need to ward off this tendency and play the skeptic. This is what Melissa was doing when she reread her draft and asked herself, 10,000 bananas in 40 years? Really? If a claim seems too good to be true, it is your job to verify it. This is especially important when that amazing "fact" that you've just stumbled upon confirms your perspective.

Playing the skeptic can be challenging for two different reasons.

First, as human beings, we are often quite attached to our existing perspectives. Stepping back from our beliefs, examining them objectively, and considering the potential validity of opposing points of view can at times lead us to the discomfiting position of questioning not only the factual basis of our beliefs and opinions, but also our own identities. While this can be difficult, you must consider that an untested perspective is tantamount to having blind faith. Testing your beliefs as a skeptic can lead either to a change in your perspective or to a re-confirmation of it.

The second reason why playing the skeptic is challenging is more of a practical concern: it takes time. To play the skeptic, don't rush, consider plausibility, crosscheck with other sources, and do the math.

Don't Rush

As Melissa discovered in the example above, coming back to her draft only one day later allowed her to step back from her source and evaluate it with fresh eyes. Also, because she was drafting well ahead of her deadline, she had the time to verify the statement about banana 10,000. If you're writing a paper the day before it's due, it's unlikely that you'll have the time to evaluate your sources effectively.

Karma was surprised to read in a student's grant proposal that only one in five adults have a high school diploma; that number seemed unbelievable, so unbelievable that she went to her student's source, which says, "It might surprise you to know that one in five working adults today lack a high school diploma" (Trask). She isn't sure whether her student was reading too fast or writing too fast, but the student accidentally ended up saying the exact opposite of what the source did.

Consider Plausibility

If you come across a statement that seems too good or outrageous to be true, it's time to consider whether it's plausible. As neuroscientist Daniel J. Levitin points out, considering plausibility is akin to using your common sense; you check claims against "your real world knowledge [and] observations acquired over a lifetime" (4). After considering it for a day, it just didn't seem plausible to Melissa that she had eaten 10,000 bananas in her lifetime.

It's worth noting, however, that implausible things do sometimes occur. In 1974, without permission of New York City authorities, the French tightrope artist, Philippe Petit, strung a wire between the twin towers of the World Trade Center. Much to the astonishment of pedestrians 1,000 feet below, he then walked back and forth between the two towers. That feat might seem implausible based on your real-world knowledge (your common sense might tell you that no one should attempt such a stunt) but it happened, and Petit survived to tell the tale.

The point is that while you can't dismiss information or claims based entirely on common sense, when your common-sense alarm bell starts ringing, it's time to dig a bit further. The burden to verify is on you.

Crosscheck with Other Sources

If you learned of Petit's stunt from an acquaintance and you were playing the skeptic, you could easily verify the truth. You might look to the many newspaper articles that reported the event in 1974, view a documentary film produced in 2008 (*Man on a Wire*), and see footage of it on *YouTube*. In so doing, you would be engaged in a practice common among effective researchers: crosschecking your sources.

Most newsworthy events are reported by a number of different sources, and you can take advantage of this to make sure that you have the facts straight. Perhaps, after a recent flood, you read in a newspaper that there have been 500 fatalities. Before including this number in your own essay, you should check to see if other newspapers are reporting the same number. If four different newspapers confirm this number, and a fifth newspaper records only 50, then you might reasonably conclude that 500 is the correct number. However, before you dismiss the fifth source as unreliable, you need to take one more step: check the publication date. If the fifth article was published two days after the flood and the others were published two weeks later, it's possible that they were equally trustworthy given the information available at the time of publication. Reported death tolls often change in the weeks and months following a disaster.

Examining different sources on the same subject can also give you a sense of the different perspectives that shape the way a subject is presented. While ethical journalists working for reliable media aim to report events objectively, the venues where they publish their articles can impact the choices they make with regard to how they frame the event. A front-page reporter on the flood may emphasize the number of fatalities that resulted, a financial pages reporter may focus on how much it will cost to repair the damaged infrastructure, and a science-page reporter might zero in on how this flood is related to climate change.

The proliferation of sources in the age of the internet has made it more essential than ever for writers to check their sources, but the internet has also made it easier to conduct a crosscheck. For instance, many large circulation newspapers and magazines maintain digital archives of their articles, which can be accessed for free. There are also a number of reliable fact-checking organizations that you can turn to for verification. *Politifact* and *FactsCan* investigate and rate the truthfulness of politicians' claims in the US and Canada, respectively, and the Associated Press publishes an online column called *Not Real News: A Look at What Didn't Happen Last Week*, in which they review fabricated or partially true stories that were reported as real news in the previous week. *Snopes* checks news and rumors alike. In addition, the Committee for Skeptical Inquiry brings scientific expertise and rational thought to bear in their investigations of fringe science claims.

Do the Math

In *A Field Guide to Lies*, Levitin asks his readers how they would evaluate the following hypothetical claim: "In the thirty-five years since marijuana laws stopped being enforced in California, the number of marijuana smokers has doubled every year" (4).

When we have presented this claim to our students and given them a few minutes to figure out how to evaluate it, they immediately go to the internet. Some try to find a source that records the number of pot smokers in California today and 35 years ago. Some try to find evidence that marijuana laws were actually relaxed 35 years ago. These are logical steps one might take to evaluate such a claim, but in this instance, our students make the evaluation more complicated than it has to be.

All one really needs to put this claim to rest is a calculator.

As Levitin explains, if you assume that there was only one pot smoker in California 35 years ago (certainly a gross underestimation) and you double that number for each year since then, by the time you get to year 35, you would have a "yield of more than 17 billion—larger than the population of the entire earth" (4)!

We'll have more to say about paying attention to numbers and how they're represented in sources in later chapters. For now, we leave with you with a simple reminder: sometimes you just have to count your bananas.

E. The Three Rs in Action: A Sample Source Evaluation

For the sample source evaluation, we'd like you to read the following article, which appeared in the *New York Times* Opinion pages.

How to Stop Overprescribing Antibiotics

Craig R. Fox, Jeffrey A. Linder, and Jason N. Doctor

Antibiotics are an indispensable weapon in every physician's arsenal, but when prescribed unnecessarily for nonbacterial infections like the common cold, as they too often are, they provide no benefit and create problems. They wipe out healthy bacteria and can cause side effects like yeast infections and allergic reactions. Worse still, they contribute to the rise of "superbugs" that resist antibiotic treatment.

The Centers for Disease Control and Prevention estimates that about half of outpatient antibiotic prescriptions in the United States are unnecessary. It also estimates that each year as many as two million Americans suffer from antibiotic-resistant illnesses, and 23,000 die as a result.

Clearly, we need to get doctors to prescribe antibiotics more selectively. But how can this be done?

Several strategies have been tried in recent years, without much success. Educating doctors and patients about the proper use of antibiotics has had only a modest effect, as most doctors already know when antibiotics are called for. Alerts sent to physicians through the electronic health record reminding them to not prescribe unnecessarily are often ignored because doctors are overloaded with such messages. And offering doctors financial incentives has had mixed results, in part because the payments are modest relative to a doctor's salary.

These strategies are all based on the assumption that physicians are rational agents who will do the right thing if provided proper information and incentives. But what if doctors are a little irrational, like the rest of us? They may overprescribe antibiotics out of an unrealistic fear that the patient could eventually develop complications and need them, or because it is easier than arguing with a patient who insists on getting them. (Doctors appear to take the path of least resistance as they get more tired. In a study published in JAMA Internal Medicine, we found that prescription of antibiotics increased over the course of four-hour clinical shifts, whether or not it was called for.)

Over the last few years, our research team has developed several new approaches to reducing unnecessary antibiotic prescribing, drawing on insights from behavioral economics and social psychology. These disciplines acknowledge that people do not always behave rationally and are strongly motivated by social incentives to seek approval from others and compare favorably to their peers.

In one study published a few years ago, we asked a group of doctors to place a signed poster in their exam rooms pledging to follow standard guidelines on antibiotic prescription. This tactic, which pressured doctors to act consistently with their own publicly stated commitments, reduced inappropriate prescribing 20 percentage points relative to doctors in a control group who displayed a poster with generic information about antibiotic use.

In a more recent study, we showed that doctors tended to prescribe less aggressive medications when such options were presented more prominently (one by one, in a vertical column), with more aggressive options presented less prominently (grouped side by side, in a single category). Previous research suggested that listing alternatives individually made them appear more popular—and therefore more appropriate—than when they were grouped together. And indeed, we found that doctors were roughly 12 percent less likely to order more aggressive medications, such as antibiotics, if these options were grouped together, compared with when they were listed individually.

For our latest study, published last month in JAMA, our team gathered data on prescription rates of 248 clinicians at 47 primary care practices in Los Angeles and Boston over 18 months. Then, over another 18-month period, during which we focused on nearly 17,000 acute respiratory infection cases in which antibiotics were not called for, we tested new approaches to promoting more selective prescribing.

In one approach, doctors received a monthly email informing them of their performance relative to that of their peers. Those with the lowest inappropriate antibiotic prescribing rates were congratulated for being "top performers." Doctors who were not top performers were told "You are not a top performer." The email also included a personalized count of unnecessary antibiotic prescriptions and the count for a typical top performer. This "peer comparison" approach almost completely eliminated inappropriate prescribing: from 19.9 percent in the pre-intervention period to 3.7 percent during the post-intervention period—an 81 percent reduction.

In another approach, whenever doctors prescribed an antibiotic that was not clearly called for by the diagnosis, the electronic health record system asked them to provide a short "antibiotic justification note." The note would be entered into the patient's medical record and would be visible to others. Introducing this speed bump into the work flow, along with the prospect of social accountability, reduced the inappropriate prescribing rate from 23.2 percent to 5.2 percent—a 77 percent reduction. (Our control practices also experienced reductions, possibly because doctors knew they were being monitored, but our two approaches were much more effective.)

Taken together, our studies suggest that simple and inexpensive tactics, grounded in scientific insights about human behavior, can be extremely effective in addressing public health problems.

Craig R. Fox is a professor of management, psychology and medicine at the University of California, Los Angeles. Jeffrey A. Linder is an associate professor of medicine at Harvard Medical School. Jason N. Doctor is an associate professor of pharmaceutical and health economics at the University of Southern California.

Now that you've read the read the article, take a look at our Three Rs analysis below.

Rhetorical Situation	
Context	Physical Context: This article appeared in the *New York Times* Online on 15 March 2016. If you scrolled down to the very bottom of the webpage, you may have noticed that it was also published in the print version of the *New York Times* (*NYT*) on the same date. Social Context: By the date of this article's publication, the dangers of overprescribing antibiotics were already well known. Antibiotic-resistant infections had become part of the public conversation.
Genre	Newspaper opinion-editorial ("op-ed") article. On the website, the word "opinion" appears at the very top of the page. This means that this is not a newspaper report article, in which the author aims to inform the audience of current events from an objective point of view, but a piece in which the author expresses and supports a position. Most large-circulation newspapers have an opinion or letters to the editor section, where they print op-ed articles from members of the general public.
Audience	*New York Times* readers, who tend to be young and well educated. According to a survey by the Pew Research Center, 63 per cent of *NYT* readers are 18–49 years old and 65 per cent have a college degree.
Purpose	To inform and persuade. The authors of this article first explain the problems associated with the overprescription of antibiotics and then attempt to persuade us that they have discovered the best method for curbing this practice. Did you find this piece persuasive? If so, it might have to do with the way the authors employ rhetorical appeals.

Rhetorical Appeals	
Ethos	When we have presented this article to students, many of them have connected its ethos to its physical context. The *NYT* is a well-respected newspaper. It has been in print for over 150 years and has won 125 Pulitzer prizes for journalism, more than any other US newspaper. While anyone can submit an op-ed article to the *NYT*, the acceptance rate is very low. Only the most well-written and well-informed op-ed articles will pass the *NYT* vetting process. The authors of this article also appeal to ethos by virtue of who they are. At the end of the article, you'll see the authors' credentials: "Craig R. Fox is a professor of management, psychology and medicine at the University of California, Los Angeles. Jeffrey A. Linder is an associate professor of medicine at Harvard Medical School. Jason N. Doctor is an associate professor of pharmaceutical and health economics at the University of Southern California." They have the credibility to write about this subject. They further signal their credibility in the body of the article by indicating that they are part of the research team that tested the methods described in the article: "For our latest study, published last month in *JAMA*...." They also cite other credible sources, such as the Centers for Disease Control and Prevention.
Logos	The authors' main claim is that the methods they've tested for curbing the overprescription of antibiotics have succeeded to a significant extent. They support this claim with brief summaries of the methods and statistics of the results.
Pathos	While the presence of ethos and logos may have been enough to persuade many readers, the authors don't shy away from appeals to pathos. For instance, they use figurative language to emphasize the significance of the problem: "They wipe out healthy bacteria...and contribute to the rise of 'superbugs.'" They also cite statistics that many readers would find alarming: "...each year as many as two million Americans suffer from antibiotic-resistant illnesses, and 23,000 die as a result."
Reality Check	
Plausibility	How did this article align with your real-world knowledge? Do you know of someone who's had an antibiotic-resistant infection? Have you already heard of this problem? Has a doctor ever given you an antibiotic prescription for cold symptoms? How about the methods the authors propose? Would you be more likely to curb one of your unhealthy habits if you knew that someone was observing you, recording your actions, and comparing you to your peers?

Cross-check with Other Sources	Perhaps this is the first time you've heard about antibiotic-resistant infections. If so, an internet search could help you to verify the existence and significance of this problem, leading you to articles from other credible sources, such as the World Health Organization (WHO) and the Government of Canada, which published the "Canadian Antimicrobial Resistance Surveillance System Report" in 2017.
Do the Math	Because of the conventional length of this genre, the authors did not go into a lot of detail about their methods or how they conducted their statistical analysis. If you're skeptical about their numbers, you can use the links they provide to their research articles to learn more about their calculations.

Table 1.1

A Professional Writer Playing the Skeptic

As a final exercise in understanding how rhetorical analysis works, we encourage you to read "Facebook Isn't Making Us Lonely," by Eric Klinenberg on *Slate.com*. In this article, Klinenberg counters the thesis of another author, Stephen Marche, who argued in an *Atlantic* article that contemporary social networking habits are leading to social isolation. Although Klinenberg doesn't reference rhetorical appeals or rhetorical situation by name, he is offering a rhetorical analysis of Marche's article. After you've read Klinenberg's piece, consider the following questions:

- How does Klinenberg call attention to Marche's faulty logic and over-reliance on appeals to pathos?
- How does Klinenberg use rhetorical appeals to make his own analysis persuasive?
- Do you notice any Reality Check moves in the article?
- Does Klinenberg's argument cause you to question Marche's credibility?

CHAPTER TWO

Evaluating Academic Resources[1]

A. Introduction

It's likely that at some point in your experiences as a student you've been assigned to write a paper in which you were required to incorporate academic resources into your own argument or analysis. You may understand that academic resources are generally distinguished

---

1 In this book, we use "academic" and "scholarly" interchangeably.

from other resources because the authors are scholars and researchers working within an academic setting and that they have achieved a level of expertise within their discipline. That is, academic resources are written by people who have advanced degrees in their field and have dedicated years to studying their topics.

However, you may still have the following questions about academic resources:

- Why do I need to reference academic resources in my writing?
- What is peer review?
- What are the differences among genres of academic resources?
- What are the differences between primary, secondary, and tertiary sources?
- How should I evaluate academic resources?

In this chapter, we answer those questions so that you can make informed decisions about the kinds of resources you use.

B. Why Do We Use Academic Resources in Our Writing?

When your instructor asks you to reference academic resources in your writing, she is doing more than testing your ability to jump through some hoops on your way to a good grade. She is, rather, introducing you to a form of thinking and writing that is valued in the academic community.

Academic writers build ethos by demonstrating that they've "consulted" with experts on the topics that they're writing about. If you are not yet an expert on a topic, you can borrow ethos from writers who are already recognized experts. This is especially important for students or writers who are at the early stages of their careers. By referencing experts' publications in your own writing, you show that you have done your homework on the topic, that your ideas on the topic are informed, and, therefore, that you are yourself a reliable source of information.

Further, by reading what multiple experts have written about a single topic, you gain a sense of the academic conversation that is taking place about this subject. We realize that "conversation" may not be a word you associate with published writing. These authors aren't actually talking aloud to one another, are they? Maybe or maybe not. Academic experts do often meet, present their research, and converse with one another at professional conferences.

However, the more you read academic resources on a single subject, the more you will see that the authors of these articles and books see themselves in conversation with one another, even when they're not conversing in person. They, too, read the work of other experts and cite each other in their own writing. In fact, one of the ways experts demonstrate their expertise (and build their own ethos) is by positioning their own theories or research in relation to that of other experts (this part of a research project is called the literature review). Like you, they also have to demonstrate they've done their homework.

When you read multiple experts' writing, it is as if you are silently listening in on the conversation they've been having with one another over years and sometimes decades. When you then begin to incorporate these experts' words, ideas, and research into your own writing, you are entering the conversation. You might agree with one expert, disagree with another, or build on another writer's ideas with your own. You can't do that effectively or ethically, however, if you haven't first given your full attention to what they have to say.

It's worth noting that while academic resources are defined as written by experts, not everything an expert writes is considered an academic resource. Sometimes experts choose to write other genres, such as newspaper editorials, general-audience magazine articles, or blogs because they want to reach a broader audience. We'll be addressing those writing contexts and genres in Chapter Three. Here we focus on academic resources.

C. Test Your Current Knowledge about Academic Resources

Imagine you are taking a course on English literature, and you have decided to write your end of term paper on a novel by Emily Brontë. Your instructor says you need to cite at least three peer-reviewed sources. Through your library search, you find a journal called *Brontë Studies*, which has been tagged by the library database as a "peer-reviewed" publication. Next, you open a recent issue and look at the table of contents (Figure 2.1).

Here's your test: which of the items listed in the table of contents would fulfill your instructor's requirement for peer-reviewed sources?

Volume 43, Issue 4

Editorial
Amber Adams
271–272[2]

ARTICLES
An Anne Brontë Whodunit
Sue Lonoff
273–283

The Several Stages of Gondal
Edward Chitham
284–299

Rooms in *Wuthering Heights*
Graeme Tytler
300–310

---

2 Are you wondering why the page numbering begins at 271 instead of 1? It's common practice to use consecutive numbering across all issues in a single volume. This is issue 4 of volume 43. Issue 1 of volume 43 begins with page 1.

---

3 Do the quotation marks in this title strike you as odd? If so, it's likely that you're an American reader. *Brontë Studies* is published in England where single quotation marks are used in situations when American writers would use double quotation marks. Here and in the next article on the Table of Contents, the authors are using single quotation marks to indicate that they have incorporated the coined terminology and the phrase of other authors into their titles.

Elmet. By Fiona Mozley; and *Ill Will: The Untold Story of Heathcliff.*
By Michael Stewart.
Peter Cook
362–364

*In the Footsteps of Emily Brontë: A Catalogue of the Art Work of
Percy J. Smith, Emily Brontë and* Wuthering Heights. Hertfordshire:
The Percy Smith Foundation, 2016. iv, 28 pp. No price. No ISBN.
Carolyne Van Der Meer
365–367

Figure 2.1   Table of contents
Source: *Brontë Studies: The Journal of the Brontë Society,* 2018

If your answer to this question is "Any of these items would be
suitable. They've been published in a peer-reviewed journal," you
would be wrong. Not everything published in a peer-reviewed journal
actually goes through the peer-review process (which we discuss at
length in the next section). Although it is sometimes difficult to tell
the difference based on the table of contents alone, the *Brontë Studies* editors make it fairly easy for you: all of the peer-reviewed articles
(works of original research) are listed under the category of "Articles."

Other items in the table of contents include a brief introduction ("Editorial") to the volume written by the journal's editor,
Amber Adams, as well as texts you would find helpful in your quest
to learn more about Emily Brontë, though they are not works of
original research. For example, "A Brontë Reading List: Part 9," is
an annotated bibliography; it offers brief summaries of research
articles and books on the Brontë sisters[4] that have been published
recently. The bibliography could be a good source for you in terms
of helping you to find peer-reviewed articles published in journals
other than *Brontë Studies.*

This issue also includes five book reviews. The purpose of a
book review is to help readers decide if they want to read the books.

---

4 As you may have gathered from the titles in the table of contents, there
   were three Brontë sisters, Charlotte, Emily, and Anne.

Book reviews give a brief synopsis of the book, identify its central themes (in the case of literary texts) or its contributions to a field of knowledge (in the case of academic works), and offer an overall evaluation. If you plan to write your paper about Emily Brontë's novel *Wuthering Heights*, reading the book reviews by Bob Duckett and Peter Cook might help you to decide if it would be useful for you to read Michael Stewart's book about Heathcliff, a character from the novel. Journal editors typically assign book reviews to people who have some expertise related to the subject; however, book reviews do not go through the peer-review process, so you wouldn't be able to count these texts among your three required sources for your assignment.[5]

The editors of *Brontë Studies* distinguish the different types of texts they publish by the categories on the table of contents. They also indicate which texts are peer-reviewed (only the articles) in their statement of "Aims and scope," which appears on the journal's homepage:

> *Brontë Studies* is the only journal solely dedicated to research on the Brontë family. Published continuously since 1895, it aims to encourage further study and research on all matters relating to the Brontë family, their background and writings, and their place in literary and cultural history. Original, peer-reviewed articles are published as well as papers delivered at conferences, notes on matters of interest, short notices reporting research activities and correspondence arising from items previously published in the journal.

In other journals, the categories may be less clear, and you may need to delve a bit further into the issue to ascertain the differences between the various types of text they publish. We find that our students are more prone to confusing book reviews (as opposed to other journal offerings) with research articles, so we've provided you with a few more tips on how to tell the difference.

---

5 That doesn't mean you can't cite the book review in addition to your three peer-reviewed articles.

Book Review or Research Article?

If distinguishing a research article from a book review seems a bit confusing, don't worry. There are a few things you can look for to tell the difference:

- The title of a book review often has the word "review" in it.[6]
- The writer of the review and the author of the book being reviewed are both typically named at the top of the review and in the table of contents.
- Book reviews are shorter than research articles. For example, Duckett's review of Stewart's book is only three pages long.
- Research articles tend to reference many other sources and have a lengthy list of works cited at their conclusion. Book reviews will include fewer references and have shorter works cited lists. In "Blurring Boundaries and a Generic Matrix in *Jane Eyre*'s 'Political Unconscious,'" Robab Khosravi cites the work of 20 other writers, whereas Duckett cites only one source—the book he is reviewing.

In the coming sections, we'll be discussing different types of academic sources, which will help you further understand what distinguishes one academic genre from another, but first we have an explanation of the peer-review process.

D. Peer Review

Peer review is the process by which an academic author's writing is evaluated and either accepted for publication or rejected. Both research articles and some book-length scholarly works (sometimes referred to as "monographs") go through the peer-review process

---

6 A literature review, which is another animal entirely, also often has the word "review" in the title. We'll cover that later in this chapter.

before they are accepted for publication. Understanding how the process works may give you some insight into why your instructor may insist upon you citing peer-reviewed sources in your paper. Below, we describe the process as it relates to a research article, though it is largely the same for a scholarly book.

Vocabulary Note

Sometimes journals use the word "refereed" instead of "peer-reviewed" to indicate that research articles have been reviewed by disciplinary experts prior to publication. Don't let the vocabulary trip you up. "Peer-reviewed" and "refereed" mean the same thing.

The Peer-Review Process

After an author submits his research article to a journal, the journal's editor determines whether it is suitable for the theme and scholarly scope of the journal. This initial screening is one of the duties Karma performs in her role as the editor of the *Margaret Atwood Studies Journal*. Imagine for instance that Karma received an article on the short stories of Alice Munro. Unless the article drew significant connections between Munro's and Atwood's works, no matter how well written, Karma would send it back to the author with the suggestion that the article would be better suited for another journal. On the other hand, if the article was indeed related to the works of Margaret Atwood, Karma would then send it on to a group of two to three reviewers.

The reviewers are considered "peers" because they are experts on the same subject; that is, they share scholarly interests with the author. For instance, reviewers for the *Margaret Atwood Studies Journal* are academics who also study the works of Margaret Atwood or contemporary Canadian literature. Peer reviewers are selected because their expertise enables them to offer an informed evaluation of the article.

Each reviewer reads the article and writes a brief evaluation of it that includes a recommendation to the editor: publish, reject, or revise and resubmit. To ensure that the peer-review process is objective and unbiased, most journals employ a *double-blind protocol*. This means that the author's name does not appear on his article when it is sent for review, and the reviewers' names are withheld from their evaluations.

The reviewers' recommendations are based on a number of criteria. While the criteria may vary to a certain extent based on the academic discipline in which the journal is situated, they generally include the following:

- Does the article uphold the scholarly standards of the journal and the discipline?
- Does the article contribute new, original arguments, theories, or research that will advance the scholarship in the discipline?
- Does the author's argument proceed based on rational thinking and logical deductions (i.e., does it appeal to logos)?
- Does the author present enough evidence to support his argument or results persuasively?
- Has the author taken into consideration what other experts have contributed to research on this topic?
- Has the author used research methods accepted by the discipline?
- Is the article free of grammatical errors and stylistically fluid?
- Is the article written in the format that is the accepted convention for the discipline?

After the journal editor receives the peer reviewers' evaluations, she makes a decision to publish or reject the article or invite the author to revise his article based on the written evaluations and resubmit it. In any case, the reviewers' written evaluations are returned to the author so that he can better understand why his article has been accepted, rejected, or how he can improve the article if the final recommendation of the review is "revise and resubmit."

By the time you read a peer-reviewed article or book, it has been read and given the stamp of approval by at least three or four experts, and thus, it has credibility. In other words, the peer-review system has done the first level of evaluation work for you. This is why referencing peer-reviewed sources in your own writing enables you to appeal to ethos and, therefore, make your own argument more persuasive. However, this does not mean you have no evaluation work to do. Even after finding a number of peer-reviewed sources, you will still need to determine whether each source is appropriate for your argument.

Playing the Skeptic: Predatory Journals and Fraudulent Research

Peer review is kind of like being tried by a jury of one's peers, though with less dire consequences if the decision doesn't go your way, although we know a few pre-tenured professors who would disagree with that last clause.

The peer-review process is rigorous and time intensive. It can also be stressful for academic authors because much depends upon the outcome of the review. You may have heard the phrase "publish or perish." It refers to the fact that publishing research articles and scholarly books is a condition of employment for most professors. If a professor does not publish, she may lose her job or be denied promotion. And, for the most part, the only publications that count are those that have gone through peer review.

Consider that the next time one of your professors seems particularly harried. You know how impatient and anxious you sometimes feel when you're waiting to get your paper back, hoping for a high grade. Imagine waiting, often for months, to learn whether your article has made it through the peer-review process.

We're not telling you this to induce you to empathize with your professors (that would be an appeal to pathos) but to help you understand the stakes involved and, following from that, why the peer review system sometimes fails or is abused.

Predatory Journals

Recently, Melissa received an email from a journal inviting her to submit a paper she'd presented at an academic conference. Fortunately, she could tell immediately that the email had come not from a real peer-reviewed journal, but from a "predatory journal," thus named because such journals prey upon young and inexperienced academics who are desperate to have their articles published.

Do you see the signs that this is a predatory journal in the first few sentences of the email Melissa received?

Dear Melissa Bender,

This is *Journal of Modern Pedagogy Review*[7] ..., a professional journal published worldwide by Stellar Scholar Publishing Company, New York, NY USA.

We have learned your **"Learning at the Threshold: WAC Practices for Inclusive Education" at 13th Biennial Conference of the Association for Academic Language and Learning(AALL2017).** We are very interested to publish your paper in the Journal of Modern Pedagogy Review. If you have the idea of making our journal a vehicle for your research interests, please send the electronic version of your paper to us through email attachment in MS word format. All your original and unpublished papers are welcome.

Hope to keep in touch and publish some papers or books from you and your friends in USA. As a Stellar Scholar publishing group, we wish to become your friend if necessary.

Did you notice a few ungrammatical phrases ("we have learned your" and "interested to publish") and the absence of articles[8]

---

7   We've changed some of the identifying details in this example, such as the titles of the journal and the publishing company, but the remaining wording is true to the email that Melissa received.

8   Such as, "the," "an," or "a."

before some nouns? Did you find the writer's wish to become Melissa's friend "if necessary" as comical as she did? These lapses in the conventions of the English language indicate that English is not the writer's first language, and while Melissa fully admires the linguistic dexterity of multilingual individuals, she also knows that the editors at a legitimate academic journal based in the US would not send out an email with errors. Further, the fact that the journal welcomes "all your original and unpublished papers" is a red flag, suggesting that they aren't very selective about what they publish, even though the email later claims that submitted articles are peer-reviewed.

Predatory journals, which have become more common in recent years, send out mass emails to academics, touting a speedy peer-review process and offering to publish articles for an "article processing fee." In fact, they are only money-making scams and don't employ a peer-review process at all. They will publish any article, as long as the author has paid the fee. To appear legitimate, predatory journals frequently list the names of real academics as members of their editorial review board, even though those individuals have never been asked to review articles for the journal and are typically unaware that they've been named on the journals' websites (Pettit).

A few years ago, Mark Shrime, a medical researcher at Harvard University, set out to prove just how indiscriminant and unethical these journals can be. As reported by Elizabeth Segren, a writer at *Fast Company*, Shrime created a nonsense article using a program that generates random text, gave it a nonsensical title, "Cuckoo for Coco Puffs? The surgical and neoplastic role of cacao extract in breakfast cereals," and submitted it to several suspect journals using irreverent pseudonyms.[9] Even though the article made no sense, 17 journals accepted the article on one condition: that the author pay a "processing fee" of $500.00.

Students come across these fake journals all the time, because the journals are open-access and thus accessible through Google.

---

9 Want to see just how nonsensical this article is? See the link to the pdf at the end of Elizabeth Segren's article.

That's why we advise starting your research through your library subject guides (we talk about that more in Chapter Five).

Unfortunately, many naïve or inexperienced academics have fallen victim to the practices of predatory journals, despite the fact that it is fairly easy to test the legitimacy of a journal. Consider these questions if you suspect that an article you've found was published in a predatory journal.

- Is the title of the journal oddly redundant? A legitimate journal might be titled *The Journal of X* or *The Review of X*, but use of both "journal" and "review" by *The Journal of Modern Pedagogy Review* suggests either that the journal's "editors" didn't have command of the English language or that they were aiming primarily for search engine optimization.
- Is the title of the journal too broad? Does the title suggest that it covers everything in all social science fields, for instance? How would a title like that appeal to a specialized audience of academic experts?
- What happens when you type the title into a search engine? Does the word "scam" or "fraud" come up immediately? When Melissa followed such links for *The Journal of Modern Pedagogy Review*, she found many academics complaining about the illegitimacy of the journal and its unethical practices.
- Is the journal's website sparse? Are there many grammatical errors? Does the design of the website look unprofessional? Are its links inoperable or do they lead to sites unrelated to the journal?
- While you're on the website, consider the journal's scope. Does it seem too broad? Does it claim, for instance, to publish articles on anything from anthropology to public administration? Again, it's helpful to remember who the intended audience is for academic journals: specialists who are looking for the work of other specialists in their own discipline.
- Examine the submission guidelines on the website. Do they mention that the authors need to pay a fee to publish? Legiti-

mate peer-reviewed journals do not require their authors to pay a fee, and they are not money-making ventures. They cover their costs through individual and library subscriptions and sometimes through grants.

Fraudulent Research

Although the peer-review system is designed to ensure that only high-quality, ethically conducted research makes it to print, sometimes the system fails to filter out faulty research or results that have been purposefully skewed.

The most notorious example of this is a study published by a British physician, Andrew Wakefield, who claimed to have discovered a causal link between the measles, mumps, and rubella (MMR) vaccine and the onset of autism in children (1998). After the study was published in *The Lancet*, a well-respected, peer-reviewed medical journal, other researchers were unable to replicate the results of the study, and Wakefield was found to have falsified his data for monetary gain.

Although *The Lancet* retracted the article, Wakefield lost his medical license, and medical researchers thoroughly debunked the supposed connection between the MMR vaccine and autism, the damage had already been done. The original study received such sensationalized media attention that it inspired the anti-vaccination movement. Now physicians sometimes have a difficult time convincing some parents to have their children vaccinated.

Does the existence of predatory journals and fraudulent research mean that you must question the legitimacy of every peer-reviewed source that you find? Not necessarily.

As awareness of predatory journals grows, many library systems have begun to weed such journals out of their databases, and academics have published articles warning others about their practices.[10] Since the Wakefield controversy, many journals like *The Lancet*, which stake their reputations on the quality of the research

---

10 For a recently published article on the subject of predatory journals, see Emma Pettit, "These Professors Don't Work for Predatory Journals."

they publish, have doubled-down on their peer-review processes to ensure that publication of fraudulent research doesn't occur again. However, it would be remiss of us not to warn you that such problems exist in the world of peer-reviewed publishing.

E. Academic Genres

Rule number one for evaluating academic sources is "know thy genres."

You can't evaluate a source if you don't understand its genre. Moreover, as you've probably already gathered from this chapter, not all academic genres are alike, nor are they valued in the same way by academic audiences.

As we discussed in Chapter One, every genre of writing has its own conventions based on the rhetorical situation in which those genres are produced. One of the ways in which academic writers appeal to ethos is by working successfully within those conventions. In this section, we introduce you to the major genres of academic writing and their conventions.

1. Research Articles

The research article is a peer-reviewed genre in which the author or authors advance their own original research on a particular topic. While this is true of research articles across all academic disciplines, how "original research" is defined varies from one discipline to the next. Below, we overview how research is defined and conducted in the humanities versus the sciences and social sciences.

Research in the Humanities

In humanities disciplines, original research typically involves writers advancing their own arguments or interpretations of the primary sources that define their fields. For literary scholars, primary sources are texts such as novels, plays, and poetry. For historians, primary sources include artifacts from the period and region under study, such as letters written by people who lived in London during the seventeenth-century plague pandemic or the coins that were used in a remote area of China in the eighteenth century. Sculptures and paintings are examples of primary sources for art historians.

That said, humanities scholarship can often be quite interdisciplinary in terms of the use of primary sources. A literary scholar studying Wordsworth's poetry might also read the letters he exchanged with his sister, Dorothy, to better contextualize her analysis of the poems. A historian writing about the eighteenth-century Grand Tour might examine the paintings that many grand tourists purchased as souvenirs during their travels.[11]

Research in the humanities typically involves studying the primary sources, conducting library research to determine what other scholars have already written about the primary sources, and devising one's own argument about how the significance of the primary source might best be understood.

Research articles in the humanities typically include a thesis statement somewhere near the beginning of the article. The thesis statement presents the author's main argument. In the body of the research article, the author proceeds to prove the validity of this argument through analysis of his primary sources.

Overall, the writing itself constitutes the research in humanities disciplines, and the article or book that the writers compose is considered a secondary resource.

Research in the Sciences and Social Sciences

In science disciplines, such as biology and chemistry, and social

---

11 For the curious (and we hope all of our readers are curious), the Grand Tour was a tradition that started in eighteenth-century Britain, wherein wealthy young men spent time traveling on the European continent, sometimes for years, to complete their educations. The idea was that they would learn the languages, culture, and politics of the countries they visited to become more informed members of the ruling class. In reality, they often misbehaved while traveling and returned home with a renewed sense that Britain actually was far superior to Europe.

science disciplines, such as sociology and psychology, original research proceeds in a different manner. Scholars in these disciplines typically conduct experiments or studies that involve such methods as lab work, field study, animal studies, surveys, or interviews with human subjects. However, how they organize their research is informed by prior research on the subject. After the scholars conclude their research, they write and publish an article or book detailing their findings. In these disciplines, the research article *is* the primary source. We know this is confusing; that's why we've included a table further on explaining primary, secondary, and tertiary sources across disciplines.

One key difference between research articles in humanities and sciences is authorship. Humanities research articles usually have one author or sometimes two for a collaborative work. Science research articles typically name three to ten or more authors because any individual who contributed to the research is considered an author. The first author listed is usually the principle investigator (or PI), the one who initiated and organized the research.

Research articles in the sciences also look different from humanities research articles. Most scientific research articles begin with an abstract that succinctly sums up the article, followed by five sections labeled with the following subheadings: introduction, methods, results, discussion, references. This format, referred to as IMRaD, is one of the conventions of the scientific research article (see also Chapter One). Table 2.1 explains the content of each section.

Introduction	A description of the state of knowledge on the topic prior to current study, a summary of the prior research conducted on this topic, the research question that prompted the study, or the hypothesis that was tested.
Methods	A detailed description of how the study was conducted, including the materials and instruments used, the method of measuring results, the subjects (animal or human) that may have been involved in the study, and the criteria by which the subjects were selected.
Results	A summary of the main findings of the study.

Discussion	A discussion of the significance of the results and their relationship to the hypothesis.
References	A list of works cited in the paper. These are usually quite lengthy in scientific research articles. We have seen reference sections that are longer than all of the other sections combined.

Table 2.1   IMRaD format

Within each of the sections, you may find additional subheadings that further break down the subject into manageable chunks of information.

You may be asking why science researchers must adhere to such rigid formatting in their writing. The rigid format suits the purpose and the audience.

The purpose of a scientific research article is to advance knowledge on a particular research subject and to convey the results of a study to an audience of experts. Scientific research articles can be quite challenging to wade through, even for experts, due to the complexity of their highly technical content. The IMRaD format helps readers move through articles. Further, some readers may not need to read an entire article. One reader may want only to know the results of a study, for instance. Another reader may be interested in replicating the study to see if she comes up with the same result and will need to focus on the methods employed. Thus, the IMRaD format helps the audience to locate quickly the sections that are most pertinent.

If you are in a situation in which you need to find, read, and write about scientific research, the IMRaD format is your friend. It will help you to streamline your reading process and also discern if what you've found is actually a research article. If you have found an article, even if it was published in a peer-reviewed science journal, and it does not include a methodology section, for instance, it is highly likely that it is not an article about original research. As with humanities journals, many science journals publish other types of writing in addition to research articles. For instance, the *Canadian Journal of Microbiology* publishes commentary articles and letters to the editor, and *JAMA* (the *Journal of the American Medical Association*) publishes opinion pieces. These articles may impart interesting opinions and useful knowledge, but it is important to distinguish them from research articles.

2. Scholarly Books

Scholarly books, sometimes referred to as monographs, are book-length works of original research on a single, specialized subject. They are typically written by a single author or, less frequently, collaboratively written by two authors.[12] Scholarly books are more common in humanities and social science disciplines than in hard science disciplines, in which the research article carries more clout.

Like research articles, most scholarly books go through the peer-review process before they are published, and they are usually published by university presses, such as the University of Toronto Press or the University of California Press, though there are some notable exceptions. Routledge and Palgrave Macmillan, which are privately owned presses, publish scholarly, peer-reviewed books, though they are not associated with a university.

Be aware, however, that university-based and privately owned academic presses also publish other types of books, such as textbooks, which, as we discuss later in this chapter, are not considered works of original scholarship, and trade books, which are intended for a general, non-academic audience and, thus, would not be considered "scholarly."[13]

So how can you tell if the book you've found is a peer-reviewed scholarly book? Consider the following:

• Does the book have footnotes or endnotes, an extensive bibliography, and an index?

_____

12 Not everyone is able to work together as well as Karma and Melissa.
13 We are subverting the genre conventions of the textbook by including a works cited section and footnotes, to model a proper appeal to ethos.

- Does the bibliography reference a large number of other scholarly works, such as research articles published by peer-reviewed journals?
- Does the body of the book contain in-text citations?

If you're still unsure after answering the questions above, go to the publisher's website and examine how the book is presented on the site. Publishers will frequently categorize their offerings, with separate web pages for scholarly books, textbooks, and trade or general audience books.

3. Edited Collections

An edited collection is a book that presents several chapters on a single topic or theme, each of which was written by a different academic writer. Each chapter presents an article that is generally the same length as a research article published in a journal and is held to similar kinds of standards.

The editor of a collection is an academic with expertise in the topic. He is the person who sets the thematic boundaries for the collection, seeks authors to contribute chapters to the collection, finds a publisher, writes the introduction, and submits the final manuscript to the publisher. The editor is also in charge of a few less glamorous tasks, such as corralling all the authors to submit their chapters by the deadline (and you thought you were the only one with trouble meeting a writing deadline!) guiding authors through revision when needed, ensuring that all the chapters use the same citation style, proofreading the final manuscript, and creating an index. For all that work, the editor gets to see his name on the book cover and title page.

The value of an edited collection for the audience is that it assembles a variety of academic authors' points of view on a single subject. Imagine that you've decided to explore the end-of-the-world-as-we-know-it theme in Atwood's works for a Canadian literature class. You might want to seek out a collection that Karma recently edited, *Margaret Atwood's Apocalypses*, which brings together six different authors' approaches to the topic in Atwood's novels and poetry.

You'll know you're holding an edited collection if the following apply:

- The words "edited by" precede the editor's name on the book cover.
- The table of contents lists a different author's name next to the title of each chapter.

Some edited collections are peer-reviewed and others are not, depending on the publisher's protocols. If your instructor has asked that you use only peer-reviewed resources, you can go to the publisher's website to make the determination. All academic publishers' websites will include a web page for authors, which explains their reviewing and publishing processes.

4. Literature Reviews

Sometimes the jargon we academics use just doesn't make sense to a novice. The "literature review" is a case in point. In this instance, "literature" doesn't refer to poetry, novels, or drama, as it would in your English class, and a literature review (or a review of the literature, as it is sometimes called) is *not* a book review.

A literature review is, rather, an academic genre for which the author has read the existing research articles on a particular topic and then synthesizes and evaluates the findings of those articles. In other words, the research articles *are* the literature. A literature review writer typically announces that she is going to "review the literature" in the title of her article or in her introduction. Literature reviews are common in science and social science disciplines, but you will also find them in other disciplines.

The phrase *literature review* may be used for both a full standalone article and a section of a larger project. Often, the second chapter of a dissertation is a literature review. After the introduction, the writer gives a thorough discussion of literature on the topic and situates his own argument within the conversation.

At the beginning of this chapter, we proposed the idea that academic writers are in conversation with one another. You might want to think of the literature-review writer as facilitating those conversations and putting them into writing for the purpose of helping her audience contribute to the conversation or make use of existing knowledge.

The overall purpose of a literature review is to give the audience a sense of two things:

1. The current state of knowledge on a particular research topic.
2. A sense of the gaps or inconsistencies in the knowledge or the research.

An academic might turn to a literature review if he is in the process of planning his own study and needs to understand methodologies that have already been used or to learn what is still unknown about the topic so that he might fill in the knowledge gaps with his own research.

Alternatively, an academic might use the literature review to get up to speed on current knowledge in the field. Such was the case for Melissa a few years ago when she was writing a research article on popular representations of autism. While conducting her library research, Melissa found a literature review by Meredyth Goldberg Edelson, "Are the Majority of Children with Autism Mentally Retarded?: A Systematic Evaluation of the Data." In Edelson's review of 145 studies of the intelligence of autistic children, she reveals that connections between autism and mental retardation have largely been based on faulty methodologies.

Just think about how much time Melissa saved by reading Edelson's review! She did not have to read those 145 research articles herself because Edelson had done the work for her. Further, as a writing specialist, Melissa is not qualified to evaluate the methodologies employed by autism researchers, so she was able to rely upon Edelson's expertise in this area.

If you'd like to delve further into the literature review genre, you can read a sample written by one of our students and check out our analysis of the abstract from an Environmental Studies literature review on the *Who's Your Source?* website.

5. Other Academic Genres

While conducting library research for your paper, you may come across a number of other genres.

As we mentioned at the beginning of this chapter, academic writers often attend professional conferences, where they present their research to one another. Sometimes the conference organizer will gather papers from the presenters and publish them in collections known as *conference proceedings*. Although the presenters' proposals must be reviewed by the organizing committee before they are accepted for the conference, the proceedings themselves are not typically peer-reviewed prior to publication.

A *dissertation* is a book-length work of original research that a doctoral student must write to earn a PhD. Master's degree students complete a *thesis* (typically the length of a journal article) as the final step toward graduation. While dissertations and theses are accessible through library databases, they are not "published" in the traditional sense. They have not been accepted by a publishing company nor have they passed through the peer-review process, though we've known a number of graduate students who feel as though they've run the gauntlet to get their committee (comprised of professors from their universities) to sign off on their work and allow them to get their diplomas. While many graduate students later go on to publish their dissertations as books (often after considerable post-graduation revision), these will appear in your library search categorized as a book, not a dissertation.

Conference proceedings, dissertations, and theses all present original research and they may be useful sources for your own work, but do remember that they don't convey as much ethos as peer-reviewed sources.

6. Tertiary Academic Sources

Tertiary academic sources are articles or books that do not present the author's original research; instead, they summarize, explain, synthesize, and evaluate the existing research and established knowledge on a particular subject. While tertiary academic sources are written by experts, their purpose is to teach an academic subject, introduce the audience to the major concepts relevant to a particular discipline, or provide a research overview.

One tertiary academic source that you already know well is the textbook, such as this one. While the two of us are experts in the field of composition and rhetoric, we are not presenting to you our own research, but culling from our knowledge of the discipline and our decades of experience as writing instructors to help you learn to become more effective evaluators of the sources you encounter as students, readers, and writers.

Annotated bibliographies and *encyclopedias* are other tertiary sources you might encounter. An annotated bibliography lists the major books and articles on a particular topic. Each entry in an annotated bibliography provides the reader with a brief summary of the book or article and an evaluation of its quality and accuracy. Annotated bibliographies will give you a sense of the sources available on your topic and help you to decide which of the sources will be most relevant for you. Though annotated bibliographies may be published in peer-reviewed journals, they do not generally go through the peer-review process.

The word "encyclopedia" comes from the Greek language, and its translation conveys the purpose of this genre: "general education." You probably started using encyclopedias, such as *The Britannica*, when you were in primary school, but did you know that nearly every academic discipline publishes its own encyclopedia? There are encyclopedias of psychology, microbiology, anthropology, economics, and so on. The purpose of these volumes is to convey, in the broadest of brushstrokes, the major concepts, methods, and sub-disciplines within each discipline. There are likewise sub-disciplinary encyclopedias. For instance, perception is one of the sub-disciplines in the field of psychology, and in the *Encyclopedia of Perception*, edited by E. Bruce Goldstein, you can find entries on topics such as binocular vision, kinesthesia, and dyslexia. Goldstein is a professor of psychology, and each entry in the encyclopedia is written by an academic who specializes in areas of perception.

Thus, you could say that the source is reliable and academic, but it is a tertiary source because the editor and writers are not advancing their own original research.

Encyclopedia entries are broad and brief, as is appropriate for their purpose. You wouldn't want to rely heavily on them for your research, but consulting an academic encyclopedia can be helpful if you're trying to figure out how to define a concept or understand a methodology introduced in a research article.[14] Effective encyclopedia entries also include brief reference lists, which could lead you to some useful primary and secondary sources.

If your head is swimming with all of the references we've made to primary, secondary, and tertiary sources, don't worry. It can be confusing (even for us academics) because there are disciplinary differences in the ways that we understand these categories. For this reason, we're providing you with the handy guide in Table 2.2, which presents examples of primary, secondary, and tertiary sources across five academic disciplines. In the fifth column, you'll also find examples of reliable, non-academic sources on the same subjects. While we can't cover every discipline, this table should give you a sense of categorical differences. If you're unsure about how your discipline categorizes a source you've found, you should check with your instructor.

Discipline	Primary	Secondary	Tertiary	Reliable, Non-academic Sources
Literature	Genre: novel	Genre: scholarly book	Genre: academic encyclopedia	Genre: general interest magazine article
Examples	Jane Austen, *Sense and Sensibility*.	Margaret Anne Doody, *Jane Austen's Names: Riddles, Persons, Places*.	Kirstin Olsen, *All Things Austen: An Encyclopedia of Austen's World*.	Nicholas Dames, "Jane Austen Is Everything."
Art History	Genre: painting	Genre: peer-reviewed journal article	Genre: textbook	Genre: news website article

---

14 Yes, we know about *Wikipedia*, and no, it is not an academic encyclopedia, for reasons that we'll explain in the next chapter.

Examples	Leonardo da Vinci, *Mona Lisa*, 1503.	Claus-Christian Carbon and Vera M. Hesslinger, "On the Nature of the Background Behind *Mona Lisa*."	Stephen Campbell and Michael Cole, *A New History of Italian Renaissance Art.*	Sheena McKenzie, "*Mona Lisa*: The Theft That Created a Legend."
Education	Genre: survey data	Genre: dissertation	Genre: annotated bibliography	Genre: online newspaper article
Examples	W. Wayne Young, PECTAC (Parental Expectations of Collegiate Teaching and Caring), a survey of 475 parents of college students.	W. Wayne Young, *Parent Expectations of Collegiate Teaching and Caring.*	Wayne F. Pricer, "At Issue: Helicopter Parents and Millennial Students, an Annotated Bibliography."	Sue Shellenberger, "Taking a Closer Look at Helicopter Parenting."
Environmental Studies	Genre: peer-reviewed journal article	Genre: literature review	Genre: academic encyclopedia entry	Genre: newspaper article
Examples	Gokhan Eglimez, Serkan Gumus, and Murat Kucukvar, "Environmental Sustainability Benchmarking of the US and Canada Metropoles."	Matthew Cohen, "A Systematic Review of Urban Sustainability Assessment Literature."	K.C. Samir, "Human Population Stabilization."	Paul Attfield, "Growing Cities Struggle to Stay Green."
Public Health	Genre: peer-reviewed journal article	Genre: professional health organization report	Genre: academic handbook	Genre: science news website article
Examples	V.G. Mussah et al., "Performance-based Financing Contributes to the Resilience Services Affected by the Liberian Ebola Outbreak."	World Health Organization, *Ebola Virus Disease: Democratic Republic of Congo, External Situation Report 16.*	Wolfgang Ahrens and Iris Pigeot, *Handbook of Epidemiology.*	Helen Branswell, "Ebola Outbreak in DRC Sets Up Another Test for Experimental Treatment."

Table 2.2 Primary, secondary, and tertiary sources by discipline. Complete citations for each of the sources in this table can be found in the Works Cited list.

F. How to Use Academic Sources Ethically and Effectively

Selecting the right academic resources is an important first step toward using them effectively in your own writing. Too often, we see students using resources that are only vaguely related to their topic, usually because they've underestimated how long it will take to find appropriate resources or they're easily frustrated by the search (a subject that we take up in Chapter Five).

Remember that the point of using resources in your paper is to take part in the conversation that's going on about your topic. You can't do that if you and your source aren't talking about the same issues or if your sources are engaged in different conversations.

Imagine you're hosting a party, and you overhear the following exchange between two of your guests:

Guest A: "Have you ever noticed how many Honda Civics there are in the student parking lot?"
Guest B: "Toyota Priuses get better gas mileage."
Guest A: "I counted 27 Civics in the lot this morning."
Guest B: "According to *Car and Driver Magazine*, the new Prius gets 54 miles per gallon."

Sure, these two guests are both talking about cars, and they're both citing evidence to support their points, but they aren't engaging in a conversation. They're just advancing their own arguments side by side while failing to communicate with one another. As the party host, it would be hard for you to get involved and add your own thoughts because the conversation is simultaneously going in two different directions. There's no evident connecting point.

We've seen papers from students that look like the above exchange. Usually, it's because these students have thrown together the first resources that they've found just to meet their instructors' requirement for a certain number of resources. This is not an effective strategy.

In Chapter Eight, we'll discuss at greater length how to avoid this problem. For now, it might be helpful to think about being more selective about whom you invite to your metaphorical party. It's your party/essay, so it's your job to invite the right people and keep the conversation going. If you can't figure out how to draw connections between your sources' points, your audience certainly isn't going to follow the conversation.

In the process of selecting your resources, you'll also need to read them carefully, and this takes time. Use the Three Rs strategy as your guide (see the sample source evaluation in the next section), and ask yourself:

- For humanities resources: What is the thesis? What kinds of evidence does the writer use to support that thesis? Does the writer take into consideration what other authors have written about this topic?
- For science or social science resources: What is the research question or the hypothesis that the study was testing? What were the major findings of the study?
  - Do the authors reveal any sources of funding for the research? Many scientific studies are funded through research grants, and you can typically find this information near the end of a research article.
  - Funds coming from government entities, such as National Institute of Health in the US or the Natural Science and Engineering Council of Canada, generally support research that has the potential to benefit the population at large.
  - On the other hand, some corporations invest in research that has the potential to benefit the corporation. For instance, pharmaceutical companies often fund pharmacological research, which may cause you to question the reliability of the results.
- Are there any key terms in the resource that you don't fully understand? If so, you may want look for them in an academic encyclopedia.

- Have you taken note of the authors' areas of expertise? (i.e., do you know why they're credible sources of information?)

By using the Three Rs strategy and addressing the questions above, you will be better equipped to incorporate academic resources effectively *and* ethically into your own writing. You will be able to do the following things that your instructor is likely to look for when evaluating your essay:

- Accurately summarize the main ideas of your sources. Misrepresenting an author's ideas is unethical. Failing to summarize the main ideas clearly and accurately makes your writing ineffective because your readers aren't clairvoyant. They won't know what you've read unless you tell them.
- Engage with an author's ideas and insert them into the conversation because you fully understand those ideas.
- Introduce the author's name (ethically, you must give credit to every author whose work you quote, paraphrase, or otherwise reference) as well as her area of expertise.

If it's not clear to you why the latter is important, consider the following example:

According to Joe Schmoe, "All infants should receive the MMR vaccine, unless they have compromised immune systems" (127).

The student who wrote this sentence is doing her ethical duty by naming the author, enclosing his words in quotation marks, and concluding with an in-text page citation. Why should a reader trust Joe Schmoe's recommendation, though? If you are quoting him in your essay, and you want your readers to trust you—if you want to be an effective writer—you need to show your readers why they can trust your sources:

According to Joe Schmoe, MD/PhD, Professor of Pediatric Medicine at Columbia University, "All infants should receive the MMR vaccine, unless they have compromised immune systems" (127).

That's right; you can appeal to ethos by adding a simple clause immediately after your source's name that indicates his expertise. This little clause has a name; it's an appositive. Please note that when you insert an appositive into your sentence, it needs to be enclosed in commas.

One of Karma's students recognized how important setting up sources could be when another student said it seemed like she was favoring one over the other because of how she set them up. Here's how the student responded to her classmate's critique:

She names my frequent mention of the differing opinions of Martin Filler and Jeffery F. Hamburger. She is definitely correct in stating the way I've lined my sources' credibility up has hurt the persuasiveness of my argument. I only mention [that] Filler is an architecture critic while I mention that Hamburger is a Harvard professor. In actuality, Filler is an accomplished architecture critic who has been featured in many established architecture journals since the 1980s and has written many acclaimed publications. I was too concerned with establishing credibility at all when setting up my sources to realize that the level and type of credibility listed can also support or hurt the position that I am arguing.

G. The Three Rs in Action: A Sample Source Evaluation

Using the Three Rs strategy will help you to understand your resources thoroughly and therefore be in the position to use them more effectively in your own essay. For the sample-source, three-part evaluation exercise, we'd like you to take a look at the article, "Effect of Behavioral Interventions on Inappropriate Anti-biotic Prescribing Among Primary Care Practices: A Randomized Clinical Trial" by Daniella Meeker et al., which you can access at the following URL: https://jamanetwork.com/journals/jama/fullarticle/2488307.

If you were going to reference this article in your own essay, you would need to read the entire article, but for the purposes of this exercise, you can learn a lot by reading only the abstract and introduction and scanning the formatting. Do that now, and then look at what we have to say below about the Three Rs.

Rhetorical Situation	
Context	*Physical Context*: This article appeared in *JAMA* (the *Journal of the American Medical Association*) on 9 February 2016. *Social Context*: As with the article you read for the rhetorical analysis in Chapter One, this article appeared at a time when the overprescription of antibiotics was a growing concern for the public, as well as among healthcare professionals.
Genre	Peer-reviewed research article. *JAMA* indicates on its home site that it is a peer-reviewed journal. You might have also guessed that this a research article by its subtitle, "A Randomized Clinical Trial," and by the language in the abstract, in which the authors provide details on the subjects in their study and the interventions that they implemented.
Audience	Did your eyes glaze over when you got to all those numbers and percentages in the results section of the abstract? That's because you're not the intended audience for this article. This is intended for an audience of experts: other medical researchers or clinical practitioners.

Purpose	To inform and persuade. It's probably evident that the purpose of a scientific research article is to inform other members of the research community about the results of a study, but you may be questioning the role persuasion has to play in this genre. Considering how rhetorical appeals are employed in this article will help you to understand.
Rhetorical Appeals	
Ethos	The credentials that follow each author's name at the beginning of this article are the first hint of ethos. However, authors have to do a lot more than indicate their degrees to get their article published in a prestigious, peer-reviewed journal like *JAMA*. Thus, they appeal to ethos in a number of other ways. Did you notice that the article is in IMRaD format? By employing this formatting, the authors signal to journal editors and readers that they understand the conventions of the genre and that they are members of this research community. An article formatted in a different manner would likely not make it to peer review, let alone be published. Did you notice how long and detailed the methods section is? This, too, is an appeal to ethos, in that the authors are demonstrating that they've used effective methods for conducting their research and collecting data.
Logos	The authors' main claim is indicated in the first sentence of the abstract: "Interventions based on behavioral science might reduce inappropriate antibiotic prescribing." They support this claim in their results section by presenting the percentage of behavioral changes they recorded during their study.
Pathos	Though you'll see pathos less frequently in academic resources, it may be employed, especially in introductory paragraphs, to grab the reader's attention or to illustrate why the topic is worthy of notice. In this article, pathos emerges subtly in the introduction, which indicates how widespread antibiotic overprescription is and why it's a problem. They're not trying to make their readers feel empathy or fear, but, rather, to induce the reader to read the entire study.

Reality Check	You might not feel qualified to conduct a Reality Check on an article like this because of its rhetorical situation. Certainly, unless you're a statistics student, you'd likely have a hard time evaluating the calculations. However, if you're feeling skeptical, there are still a few strategies you can use to verify the reliability of this article.
Plausibility	As with the article you read for the rhetorical analysis in Chapter One, you can think about how this article, especially the introduction, aligns with your real-world experiences. Do you also think changing physician behavior is an effective approach to halt the overprescription of antibiotics?
Cross-check with Other Sources	The number of times an article has been read and cited, meaning that other researchers have referenced this article in their publications, is a good indication of how well experts regard a particular resource. At the top of the webpage for this article, you'll see an indicator of the number times the article has been viewed and cited. At the moment that we're writing this, those numbers are 49,184, and 128, respectively. That's a lot, and it will likely be more by the time you have this book. If you also click on the "Altmetric" link at the top of the page, you'll see how many times the article has been mentioned in other kinds of sources, including general audience magazines and newspapers, blogs, Twitter, and Facebook. Of course, you'd want to pay attention to who's writing these blogs and Tweets, but the overall "score" for this article is quite high: it has been referenced 496 times!

Table 2.3

H. Student Writing Sample

Did you notice some of the authors of the research article that you just examined were the same folks who wrote the op-ed article that we analyzed in Chapter One? If yes, give yourself a pat on the back right now for being an attentive reader.

Melissa asked her students to do a comparative rhetorical analysis of the two articles. Here's how one of her students responded.

Different Strokes for Different Folks: An Examination of Context-Specific Writing Strategies
Erika Gant

In order to compose an effective piece of writing, authors must ensure that their work is appropriate for their particular rhetorical situation. Not all compositions are intended for all readers. Not all genres abide by the same stylistic protocols. Authors must remain aware of the context in which they intend to present their work, in order to construct an appropriate, successful publication. As a consequence of this, a prudent reader may find distinct differences in the way different works—with different rhetorical situations—adapt their writing to match their circumstances. A powerful example of this phenomenon can be seen in two articles written on the same topic, by the same authors. "How to Stop Overprescribing Antibiotics" is a publication in *The New York Times*, intended for a general audience of online readers. "Effect of Behavioral Interventions on Inappropriate Antibiotic Prescribing Among Primary Care Practices," on the other hand, is a research paper published in the *Journal of the American Medical Association*, intended for a scientifically proficient audience. Though both articles rely on appeals to ethos to persuade the readers of the credibility of the authors and their arguments, the two publications make these appeals in very different ways.

The New York Times article is confronted with the challenge of swaying an uninformed audience. *The New York Times* readers may be unaware of the problems with antibiotic overprescription, they may not be scientifically literate, and they certainly have not ever heard of the authors. So why should they take the writers' word at face value? Why should readers believe claims that viable solutions to antibiotic overprescription have been uncovered? In a situation where a general, uninformed audience needs to be convinced, rhetorical appeals to ethos are more important than ever. The author is expected to inform the reader on the issue, *and* to persuade the reader what to think about that issue. Without a trustworthy, credible author, this type of writing cannot succeed.

In pursuit of cultivating this trust, *The New York Times* article showcases a number of scientific studies. Early in the article, the authors assert that "in a study published in *JAMA Internal Medicine*, we found that prescription of antibiotics increased over the course of four-hour clinical shifts, whether or not it was called for" (Fox, Linder, and Doctor). Immediately, the authors appeal to ethos by specifying that the research presented has been approved by an authoritative body in the field—*The Journal of the American Medical Association*. The reader is provided with a credible source and therefore a reason to believe the assertions made by the study. The authors then go on to use the personal pronoun "we," revealing themselves as the source of the study. Now they are not just a well-read conduit of information, they are established as academics—researchers published in a well-respected journal. This pattern repeats as the article moves forward: the authors do not simply present one of their publications; they do it again and again. They highlight their study on the effects of informative posters, their study on the effects of the presentation of alternatives to antibiotics, and their study on the effects of social accountability on antibiotic prescription (Fox, Linder, and Doctor). Four times the article presents published research, and all four times, that research is attributed to the writers themselves. With each iteration, the authors' credibility is bolstered. Not only are they presenting well-published studies, they are presenting a *lot* of well-published studies. Not only are the authors familiar with those studies, but they *conducted* them. The authors clearly have been working and researching their field for years, and through this presentation of several items in their body of work, they are able to demonstrate to the everyday reader that they are qualified to inform others on the specifics of their field.

This tactic of breadth over depth—while effective in establishing author legitimacy and background for a general audience—would be a less successful rhetorical appeal to ethos for a more technical, detail-demanding crowd. As such, in their research paper published in *JAMA* (a publication catered to a medically knowledgeable audience) the authors remain focused on informing readers on a single, recent study, rather than referencing the entire breadth of their works. Credibility, however, is still critically important in the pursuit of persuading an expert audience and needs to be established through some other method.

In lieu of the strategies that were effective in *The New York Times*, the *JAMA* publication makes appeals to ethos through the paper's diction choices—particularly through the use of field-specific jargon. Even before the research paper begins in earnest, the word choice in the publication's title helps to lend the paper credibility. "Effect of Behavioral Interventions on Inappropriate Prescribing Among Primary Care Practices" is a headline that is marked by clear, professional language, in accordance with the conventions of the scientific writing community (Meeker et al. 562). Terms such as "behavioral interventions," though somewhat ambiguous to the uninformed reader, are assumed to be decipherable by the specialized audience. The title is marked by the consistent use of advanced diction—particularly when compared to a title such as "How to Stop Overprescribing Antibiotics"—lending the paper a more academic tone. The result of these diction choices is a paper that immediately seems professional, scientific, and therefore more credible.

The content of the *JAMA* paper continues along this trend,

using specific diction to cultivate an impression of scientific authority. Sentences are often riddled with jargon, as can be seen in this sentence: "We performed sensitivity analyses to test for interactions between interventions by expanding the main effects model to include interaction terms for each combination of interventions and comparing this fully interacted model to the original main model using a Wald test" (Meeker et al. 565). In this example, terms not readily known by the general populace, such as "sensitivity analyses," "main effects model," and "Wald test" are left undefined, as it is assumed that both the audience and the author are familiar with these expressions. This establishment of a shared language helps to confirm that the research paper was derived from a legitimate source within the scientific community. The authors' correct use of jargon proves to an expert reader that the researchers are well educated and knowledgeable in their field. In this way, diction in the *JAMA* publication acts as a rhetorical appeal to ethos, promoting acceptance of the authors' legitimacy.

In both of these publications, the context of the work dictates the content. Composition of a convincing argument depends on the establishment of the author as a credible source of information, but the way that credibility is constructed depends on the specific circumstances in which the text emerges. An author's ability to persuade the audience hinges on his or her understanding of rhetorical situation. Audience, purpose, context, and genre must always be of forefront consideration for writers in all domains—lest their work miss the mark and fall flat.

Work Cited

Fox, Craig R., Jeffrey A. Linder, and Jason N. Doctor. "How to Stop Overprescribing Antibiotics." *The New York Times*, 25 March 2016, https://www.nytimes.com/2016/03/27/opinion/sunday/how-to-stop-overprescribing-antibiotics.html.

CHAPTER THREE

Evaluating Non-academic Resources

A. Introduction: How to Tell the Difference between Reliable and Non-reliable Resources

B. To Google or Not to Google?

C. Is *Wikipedia* Reliable?

D. How to Spot Fake News

E. Other Kinds of Non-academic Sources

F. The Three Rs and Non-academic Resources

G. How to Use Non-academic Resources Ethically and Effectively

A. Introduction: How to Tell the Difference between Reliable and Non-reliable Resources

What Is a Non-academic Source?

Non-academic sources are the sources we use every day: news, magazines, blogs, Facebook posts, tweets, and almost everything else on the internet.

A non-academic source is determined by its audience, not by

its author. If a professor writes an article about Shakespeare for a peer-reviewed journal, she is writing an academic source; the audience is presumed to be *academics*, students and other professors. If that same professor writes a murder mystery novel set in Shakespeare's Globe Theater, a blog about her favorite Shakespeare sex jokes, a tweet about how the new production of *The Tempest* set on a space station is innovative but confusing... or almost anything other than an academic book or journal article, then she has created a non-academic source. We academics might read it, but these sources are meant for a wider audience, one that doesn't have to have specialized academic language or knowledge to understand it.[1]

Why Might We Use Non-academic Sources?

Non-academic sources can be used in a variety of papers, but they are most useful when the writer needs to provide evidence about what other people think about a given subject. For example, someone writing about how doctors can engage with patients who are wary of vaccines should look at what patients are saying about vaccines in chat rooms and social media. A student writing an analysis of *Black Panther* may want to talk about how audiences discussed issues of gender, family, nationalism, or race rather than only looking at what academics said. Historians use non-academic sources as primary sources. One day, people will be digging through our re-tweets and coding our emoji use, trying to understand us better. We feel sorry for them.

However, note that some non-academic sources should **not** be used, unless your paper is *about* shady sources and you're looking for examples.

---

1 Note that these sources might be for a "general audience," but that we never actually mean that a source is for "everybody." The tweet about *The Tempest* still counts on its audience reading English at a certain level (maybe middle school), after all. The author is also guessing about what her audience knows; she might presume that someone who would read a blog about Shakespeare already knows who he is and what his major plays are.

- Don't cite cheat sites. In other words, when we see you cite *SparkNotes* or *SaveMyGrade* or *WriteMyEssayForMe*, you are signaling that you don't know your audience (graders/professors) at all, that you might use these sites for even worse purposes, that you didn't find a good source and might not know how to, and that you might not have even read the book you are writing on.

Vocabulary Tip

We have frequently noted student writers' confusion regarding three words that sound alike: cite, sight, and site. "Cite" is a verb; it refers to crediting someone's ideas. "Sight" is a sense you have. "Site" is a place, like a webpage.

- Don't cite sources that don't have authors. Most reliable sources have personal or corporate/organization authors. In other words, we trust the World Health Organization (WHO). We might not know who wrote the specific page on polio eradication, but we know the staff of the WHO is responsible for it. *Poliowasmadebymartians.net*, which has no author, webmaster, contact information, sources, or date listed, is probably not a source that should be in your essay, unless the essay is "The Government Is Not Tracking This Essay: An Analysis of Contemporary Conspiracy Theories."
- Don't cite other students. If you see a paper online that looks like a paper written in grade school or college, which looks like a paper you would write, don't cite it. Many teachers have all their students post their essays on class pages. That doesn't mean they are reliable. Tiffany's essay from her 12th grade history class on the Cold War doesn't belong in your college paper. Besides, you don't know what grade she got. Tiffany's paper might have gotten an F for mixing up Khrushchev and Stalin. Why are you trusting her?

- If you're making a secular argument, don't use sacred texts as indisputable evidence. Not only will someone who believes differently not find the source credible in a secular argument, but often when people cite texts like these, they insist they can't be argued with, which becomes a logical fallacy (see Chapter Four).[2]

It's vital that you be able to tell an academic source from a non-academic one. The two most important reasons are the following:

1. When we ask for academic sources in our assignments, that's what we will accept.
2. Not understanding the difference also means you don't understand genre, which is a problem.

One of Karma's students was writing a science article in an upper-division writing class for premeds. The student referenced a piece about a new autism study, but spent time critiquing the piece, saying it was unreliable since it didn't talk about the study parameters. The student wasn't looking at the autism study, though: she was looking at a parenting blog. It's not fair to critique a non-academic source for being exactly what it set out to be.

Often, students taking a writing exam at our university commit the "lack of evidence fallacy" (see Chapter Four). They are given a non-academic piece, usually from a newspaper or magazine, and asked to respond to it. Many students argue that the piece is "wrong" because it doesn't have a works cited page. Newspapers, magazines, and most non-academic sources don't have those. It's not part of their genre conventions.

Is your source academic or non-academic? Ask yourself the following questions about the rhetorical situation of the source:

---

2 It's fine to cite the *Torah*, *Bible*, *Koran*, or *Vedas* in religious settings and arguments. You could also use them to contextualize beliefs or the history of religious thought in secular arguments—they just can't be used as definitive evidence of your position.

- Where was this published? (i.e., What is the physical context of the source?)
- What is the genre?
- Is this for a more general audience or a specialized one?
- Does this source use jargon or count on the audience having advanced knowledge in the subject?
- Does this source cite other sources? Are they academic or non-academic?

B. To Google or Not to Google?

It's best to use academic sources in academic papers, but as we've noted, sometimes non-academic sources can be useful. It is possible to find some of those sources through your library databases, especially news databases, but most people go to Google.

There are certainly benefits to Google. It's fast and readily available. Nevertheless, there are drawbacks too:

- It gives you too many results (a search for "Gandhi" yielded more than 42 million results. You're not going to read all of that. Let's be honest, most people never go past the first page).
- It gives you all the most general information first, which makes the reluctance to go past the first page even worse. Thucydides, in his fifth-century BCE text, *History of the Peloponnesian War*, might just as well have been talking about us when he wrote: "Most people, in fact, will not take trouble in finding out the truth, but are much more inclined to accept the first story they hear."
- Google tries to give you the information you want to see. That is, if you constantly click on cat pictures, no matter what you're searching for, it's going to give you many more pictures of cats in your results. However, when you're doing research, you want a broad view of opinions and interests, not just a mirror of your own.
- Google can be manipulated. Some sites can pay to have their page appear on the first page of search results. There are more subtle

ways to have your page appear higher. (Until very recently, a webpage pretending to be an educational resource about Martin Luther King Jr. was always on the first page of searches for him. The page was actually run by a white supremacist organization.)

C. Is *Wikipedia* Reliable?

Wikipedia is usually the first site that a Google search yields. That makes sense: when most people need answers to questions, they are usually looking for basic information, not specialized knowledge.

Wikipedia has advantages: it's updated regularly; it has pages on almost everything; it's quick and easy.

The disadvantages are numerous. The information on *Wikipedia* is usually too general to be useful in academic work.

Wikipedia, on its page about citing *Wikipedia*, has a warning:

> We **advise special caution when using Wikipedia as a source for research projects.** Normal academic usage of Wikipedia and other encyclopedias is for getting the general facts of a problem and to gather keywords, references and bibliographical pointers, but not as a source in itself. Remember that Wikipedia is a wiki. Anyone in the world can edit an article, deleting accurate information or adding false information, which the reader may not recognize. Thus, you **probably shouldn't be citing Wikipedia.**

Wikipedia is often wrong.[3] Biased and inaccurate information has many causes:

- Marketing. The *Wikipedia* pages for many companies are short paragraphs taken straight from the corporation's website. Marketing departments often create and "maintain" their company's *Wikipedia* pages.

---

3 As an example, this page about citing *Wikipedia* was wrong about how a wiki page would be formatted in the eighth edition of the *MLA Handbook*—the example citation was actually from the seventh edition.

- Political Bias. In 2011, an American politician, Sarah Palin, made an inaccurate statement about a historical figure, Paul Revere. Her supporters quickly started editing *Wikipedia* pages about history, changing history to reflect what Palin said. They resisted the editors' attempts to keep the pages factual, claiming that it was not *Wikipedia*'s job to determine truth. They also claimed that because reliable sources quoted Palin, they had a right to change the pages (of course, those reliable sources were not supporting Palin's view; the news stories were reporting that she made a mistake but would not retract her statement). The pages eventually had to be locked.
- Geo-political bias. Can the Turkish-language *Wikipedia* talk fairly about the Armenian genocide when it's illegal to call it that in Turkey? One of Karma's multilingual students looked into three *Wikipedia* articles on the same event, but in different languages. This is what he said about them:

Ukraine and several other western nations claim that [Holodomor, a man-made famine that occurred during 1932 and 1933 in the Soviet Union] was a genocide, but Russia has not acknowledged it as such ("Holodomor"). Due to the editing process *Wikipedia* employs and the controversial nature of this topic, it is not suitable for use in a scholarly source.

The *Wikipedia* page for the Holodomor has a number of translations, which should be mostly identical regardless of language. However, the Ukrainian and Russian versions vary significantly in connotation when translated into English. The Ukrainian article begins by describing the Holodomor as a "genocide of the Ukrainian people, organized by the leadership of the CPSU (b) and the Government of the USSR" ("Holodomor"), which is a much more polarized introduction than the English version. The English article acknowledges that the Holodomor was a great tragedy for Ukraine, but maintains that it cannot be concluded that the Holodomor was a genocide ("Holodomor"). The Russian article is oppositely polarized, because it refers to the Holodomor as "the famine in the

Ukraine" ("Holodomor"). Its introductory paragraph also states that "In Ukraine, the mass famine of 1932–1933 was named 'holodomor,' which may imply a deliberate extermination by hunger" ("Holodomor"). The connotation of the Russian article is subtle, but it is clear that the article strongly implies that a genocide did not occur. These translations have established that the topic is a point of contention and that state interests may be fueling misinformation.

- Honest mistakes. Hey, these happen.
- Trolls. Some people change information on the internet just to mess with us. In Spring 2012, one of our friends, Denise, was teaching "The Story of an Hour." Denise checked *Wikipedia* before she wrote her quiz—to make sure students couldn't pass the quiz by just reading *Wikipedia*—and she discovered that the story summary was incorrect. The ending had been depicted as pornographic, but in a confusing way—the troll who had changed the *Wikipedia* entry probably had never actually had sex. Happily, Denise's students got perfect scores on their quizzes. They had clearly read the story and not the *Wikipedia* entry, so they were able to answer the only question on the quiz: "How does the story end?" She showed the students what would have happened if they'd relied on *Wikipedia*, however.

Evaluating *Wikipedia* Pages

- Check the last update date.
- Is the page locked? (If so, it's more reliable.)
- Is it relatively free from grammar errors?
- Are there citations for claims?
- Do those citation links work?
- Double check with other sources (you should probably just use those sources instead of *Wikipedia*).
- Look at the edit page, to see how often it's being edited, whether it's a frequent victim of scammers, etc.

D. How to Spot Fake News

There's a lot of fake news out there. In Spring 2018, a website claimed that a Canadian law protecting trans people against hate crimes would mean that citizens could be jailed for incorrect pronoun use. That simply wasn't true, and the Associated Press wrote an article debunking the false claim. The original article was probably written by someone who wanted to stoke more fear about trans people and LGBTQIA rights.

Sometimes, though, news sites are wrong because their reporters aren't trained journalists and don't fact check their stories. For example, Karma was pleased but confused once by a short article about her *Simpsons* course on *Craked.com*. It's true she teaches that course. However, the picture accompanying the article (see Figure 3.1) was of Denise Du Vernay, who co-wrote a book on *The Simpsons* with her.

Figure 3.1   Pictured: Denise Du Vernay, not Karma Waltonen

Karma was also surprised to read an article about a panel she spoke on at a ComicCon, which quoted her (Cole). She was surprised because, although she was originally scheduled to speak, she was ultimately unable to make it to the Con. So who was quoted? Surely that person wasn't pretending to be Karma. More than likely, the person who wrote the article just assumed the woman on the panel was Karma, based on an early draft of the program, without actually listening as the woman introduced herself.

Sometimes, writers don't have enough information to get news right. We then trust them, because we don't have that knowledge either, and we pass that misinformation on to others.

A few years ago, our student newspaper ran a story about how a professor was fired the quarter before she would have been eligible for a raise. The woman was fired at that time, but she wasn't a professor. The story correctly identified her as a "lecturer" the first time it mentioned her, but called her "professor" through the rest of the article. The words are often interchangeable in students' eyes. They think they're being respectful when they call us "professor," even when that's not our title. The problem here was that if she had been a professor, she could not have been fired like that. Because the student reporter (and editor) didn't know the difference between one job title and another, they couldn't understand the cause and effect in the story or the very real threats of losing a job lecturers (and not professors) face. Thus, students reading that article also wouldn't understand how a popular "professor" could be treated that way.

The first rule of spotting fake news is not to spread fake news. Always double check your sources before spreading or citing; even trusted sources and friends are fooled sometimes. Go to the original site where the story was published.

Okay, I'm at a news site. Now what do I do?

• Check the domain name. *Washingtonpost.com* is a real site. *Washingtonpost.com.co* is a fake site, designed to fool people. Beware sites with "WordPress" or "blog" in the title.[4]

---

4 Some people believe that only .edu, .gov, or .org sites are reliable. We have to evaluate all sites, regardless of domain extensions. For example, .gov site information can change based on the political party in the office (in 2017, scientific information about climate change disappeared from many United States .gov sites). The white supremacist website we refer to about Martin Luther King Jr. in this chapter is a .org. One only needs to be an organization to get that extension; the veracity or trustworthiness of the organization isn't a factor.

- Look at the layout. Is it professional?
- Look at the ads. Are they for companies you've heard of before? *BBC.com* often has ads for major car companies. *InfoWars*, on the other hand, almost exclusively has ads for *InfoWars* products, like supplements with pseudo-scientific claims.
- Do videos and ads start playing instantly? Are there tons of pop-ups? You might not be on a good site.
- Is the news divided into sections, like "sport," "national," "world," or are the news stories randomly arranged?
- Do the news stories have dates, as one would expect of a trustworthy news source?
- Do the news stories have authors and information about the authors? (Most will, though some sites, like *The Economist*, don't identify individual staff members.)
- Do the headlines seem biased, exaggerated, or slanted in a way designed to make readers angry?
- Is there an "About Us" section or a way to contact the ombudsman? (Ombudsmen are supposed to ensure that their organization's reporting is fair and unbiased. They respond to audience questions and consider all aspects of reporting, down to the language used in addressing people.)
- Is this the type of source that would have a fact checker? Traditional newspapers and magazines with long-form journalism (like *The New Yorker*) have them. Stories don't go out without being checked. If an error does happen, a retraction is printed. (The line is now blurry, though. Anyone reporting a story can claim to be a reporter, even if that person has no training in journalism or ethics. Most "news" out there now doesn't come with fact checkers or even editors.)
- Is this news actually in the news section of the paper or somewhere else? We have had students think that ads in magazines were actually articles, because the ads were designed to trick people. Be wary of cable news, too. Some of the shows are news shows, with anchors and fact checkers. Others are opinion or entertainment shows, with hosts, not reporters. The networks don't make it easy for you to distinguish between them.
- Does the site use ALL CAPS or lots of!!!!? Then it's not a good site.

As with all sources, make sure you're not drawn to the site because it confirms your own view of the world. You can also verify sites and stories through fact-checking sites like *Politifact* and *Snopes*.

It's not just Americans, of course, who fall victim to fake news. *The Globe and Mail* recently published an article about how fake news is affecting Canadian politics too (Greenspon and Owen).

Why does this matter? There are real life consequences to fake news stories. Russian interference in the 2016 US election is legendary, and it centered on fake news. The labeling of CNN as "fake" by Trump seemed like a silly bit of political positioning until Libya dismissed CNN's report of modern-day slavery (when defending itself to the international community, it said CNN couldn't be trusted, because the American President said so) (Wintour).

Satire News Sites

There's a big difference between fake news and satire sites, but they do share a commonality: people think their stories are real all the time.

Sometimes Karma shares stories from *The Onion* because they're funny, only to have unsuspecting acquaintances think they're real or to have a well-meaning acquaintance tell her that they're satire, like she didn't know.

Even when you go to a satire site, you can't always tell a satire site isn't real by using the skills listed above. Satire sites like *The Onion* and *The Beaverton* are extremely well designed. They are beautiful parodies of real news. One of Karma's students put it perfectly: "If you don't read any of the words, this looks totally true."

Sometimes, reading the words just makes someone think they're on a partisan site, or a completely reliable one, especially when the words seem plausible, if you don't know much about an issue, if you're not used to satire, or if the exaggerated headline aligns with your views.

Once, Karma saw a news post on an acquaintance's Facebook feed. It was about a religious leader coming up with a ridiculous excuse for a conservative politician's immoral behavior. For a second, she was fooled. Then, her critical-reading voice kicked in: would that leader sink that low? That couldn't be right. As soon as she started her reality check, she realized it was unreliable. The story was originally published on *The Babylon Bee*, a Christian satire site. The story was exaggerating to criticize actual religious leaders who were hypocritically defending the politician. Sadly, the exaggeration didn't go far enough, as too many readers found it believable.

Before you click "share"

- Read the whole article.
- Figure out who first published the article.
    - Was the original publisher a reputable news site? A partisan site? A satire site?
- Consider the reliability of the source.
    - Does the author rely too much on pathos?
    - Is the story too good or outrageous to be true?
    - Are the accompanying images sensational?
- Check your own impulses.
    - Are you sharing this article just because it confirms your own untested beliefs?

E. Other Kinds of Non-academic Sources

Above, we discussed the limitations of Google, but we know people are still going to use it sometimes. Besides news sites and *Wikipedia*, there are all those other millions of sites you might be tempted to use. Can we trust them?

What if someone is tweeting about himself? A man claiming to be a student tweeted about how a stranger had tweeted about seeing the student's professor grade his midterm on a plane and failing him. The student who failed and found out about it via Twitter was upset, naturally.

Except the original tweet about seeing a professor grading was likely untrue, since there was no student by that name. Moreover, the person claiming to be the named student wasn't.

You'd have to read the article on *The Washington Post*'s site (Ohlheiser and Larimer), though, to know that (or *The Chronicle of Higher Education*, where we read about this first). Most people won't. They will just retweet this little story of a person finding out he failed an exam via social media. (In the month leading up to turning this book into the publisher, Karma saw this fake story reposted several times.)

Grammar lessons on a grammar site should be correct, right?

"Everythingaboutenglish" might be trusted; the site's homepage is entitled "Everything about English for English Home Language Grade 12" and is hosted on a Weebly platform. Except we couldn't figure out who was running the site and if they knew anything about English at all. One of their pages gives this example of a "compound sentence": "He was tired. He went to bed." That is NOT a compound sentence. It's two simple sentences, sitting next to each other. On the main page, the authors have included this disclaimer:

> The information contained in this website is for general information purposes only. The information is provided by *Everything about English for English Home Language Grade 12* and while we endeavour to keep the information up to date and correct, we make no representations or warranties of any kind, express or implied, about the completeness, accuracy, reliability, suitability or availability with respect to the website or the information, products, services, or related graphics contained on the website for any purpose. Any reliance you place on such information is therefore strictly at your own risk.

Above, we mentioned not wanting to trust blog sites like WordPress, which is what Weebly is. Do the authors of the Weebly-hosted site actually have degrees in English or training in writing? Are they even more than one person, since they refer to themselves as "I" on some of the pages?

It's best to go to a reputable site for grammar. In this case, a site ending in .edu, like Purdue University's Online Writing Lab, makes more sense than trusting whatever comes up on Google when you search "compound sentences."

Most of this chapter deals with online resources, but there are certainly other forms of non-academic sources, which include newspapers, magazines, pamphlets, ads, and books. Yes—books. Very few books are academic, meaning they are written by and for scholars. In fact, most books written by scholars are still written for a general audience, and they often have the same problems that other non-academic sources have: their authors can be biased.

For example, *The Atlantic* has a critique of Gary Taubes's *The Case Against Sugar*, showing that the argument is one-sided, with many problematic claims (Engber). We have also watched John D'Agata claim that he can change whatever facts he wants, as an artist, even though he writes non-fiction. In fact, there's a book of exchanges between D'Agata and his beleaguered fact-checker, *The Lifespan of a Fact* (now a play).

In 2000, two scientists published a book claiming that men were biologically programmed to rape (nature, not nurture) (Thornhill and Palmer). The science they relied on was immensely flawed.[5] An article version never would have made it into a peer-reviewed journal. It's important to remember that most books are not peer-reviewed. Nor are they fact-checked. Just because they are written by a "scholar" doesn't mean they're reliable.

Author Michael Pollan discussed the difficulty in being reliable in a talk he gave at UC Davis many years ago, noting that when he was left on his own to fact check his books, mistakes were bound to occur, because he didn't check every single one. Like most of us, he checked the ones he had doubts about. The mistakes all occurred with facts he took for granted as true.

---

5   Margaret Wertheim did an excellent analysis of the book's flaws at *Salon.com*.

That takes us back to our own biases. Check all of your facts. Be vigilant, even when reading a source you trust or a "fact" you agree with.

In America, Howard Zinn's *A People's History of the United States* is held up as an alternative history (a real one) compared to sanitized textbooks. Recently, however, a teacher encouraged us to think critically about this source, noting,

> *A People's History* is closer to students' state-approved texts than its advocates are wont to admit. Like traditional text-books, *A People's History* relies almost entirely on secondary sources, with no archival research to thicken its narrative. Like traditional textbooks, the book is naked of footnotes, thwarting inquisitive readers who seek to retrace the author's interpretative steps. And, like students' textbooks, when *A People's History* draws on primary sources, these documents serve to prop up the main text, but never provide an alternative view or open up a new field of vision. (Wineburg)

F. The Three Rs and Non-academic Resources

This chapter has included questions about different ways to search for and evaluate non-academic sources. As you work through those questions, remember to consider the rhetorical appeals your source uses. Is he relying too much on pathos? What do you know about his credibility? Consider the rhetorical situation: the audience, purpose, genre, and context. Take a moment for a reality check.

This is a good idea even when you're searching for information that isn't school or career related.

Say you want to try online dating, but you're not sure which site to start with. A Google search might take you to *top10bestdat ingsites.com*, which lists *Zoosk* as the best. Karma actually wrote a review of *Zoosk* several years ago, and she panned it. So why does this site say it's the best? The site was created by Natural Intelligence, a marketing company that creates comparison lists as a marketing tool. In other words, *Zoosk* likely paid to have this list made and to put it in the top position.

John Oliver had a segment on his show in May 2018 about rehab centers and how difficult it is to find an effective one. He noted that one of the websites that rated centers was owned by the center in the top position.

If you don't do your Reality Check, how will you spot the ethos problems above?

If you don't check your own biases, you'll likely have problems with confirmation bias. You may have noticed people often share news reports about studies that "prove" something they want to be true. Do you use bad language? A study out there says you're more intelligent than those who don't. Do you like red wine? There's a study out there saying that's the healthiest type of alcohol for you (and there's an article debunking it) (Zeeberg). Want your depressed wife to do more housework? Studies show exercise helps with depression, but when those studies are reported in the media, they sometimes latch on to only one form of exercise: housework. Do you love the studies showing chocolate is good for you? They're funded by the Mars Company and are often reported with that gleeful bias chocolate lovers share (Belluz).

As we mentioned in Chapter One, do the math if a claim seems too good to be true or too extraordinary to be true. PBS, a trusted news source, created a *Nova* episode on anorexia in 2000. It claimed, "anorexia has been increasing by 36 per cent every five years since the 1950s." This fact, which was re-stated by other journalists and scholars, "is both factually inaccurate and nonsensical (if anorexia incidence had been increasing exponentially every five years since the 1950s, the rate would be far higher than the 1% incidence research has established)" (Radford). Anorexia is a dangerous disease, and *Nova* didn't mean to mislead its viewers, but facts matter.

G. How to Use Non-academic Resources Ethically and Effectively

Your professors prefer academic/scholarly resources, but you can't always use them. You sometimes need a news article, a blog, an interview, primary sources (like an author's diary), or even tips on good dating sites.

Sometimes, like Melissa's student who wrote about beach cruiser bikes, you need to look at Facebook to document a trend (see Chapter Eight). One of Karma's students, whose article on pet insurance was published, needed to cite legislative assembly bills, the American Pet Product Association, and a site comparing pet insurance costs (Othman).

The key is to know when and how to use them. There's a time and place for *Wikipedia*, but your evaluation of sources has to go beyond simply avoiding it. You don't want to be the student who thinks "The Story of an Hour" has a pornographic ending. You don't want to be the friend who tells her depressed friend that the only way to feel better is to do the dishes. You don't want to be the parent who was fooled by two scientists into thinking his son was a ticking time bomb of rape just because you passed down that "y" chromosome.

Thus, accept that your research just got a lot more time consuming. It's not enough to find some sources for your essay: you have to find good ones.

If it makes sense to use non-academic sources in your essay, make sure your reader has all of the information she needs to evaluate it. In addition to citing your sources, set them up for your reader. Explain who the author is, where the piece was originally published and when, what the writer wrote about and what he might have left out (and why). Further, if your audience could say, "hey, that doesn't sound reliable," engage with the counter-argument by explaining why the article needs to be considered in your essay.

CHAPTER FOUR

Logical Fallacies

A. Introduction

Every argument should consist of three appeals: logos, pathos, and ethos. These appeals may be used incorrectly (or abused purposely). Thus, we sometimes see logical fallacies.

As we discussed in the last chapter, when discussing problems with *Wikipedia*, information might be wrong for various reasons: actual mistakes, political or ideological slants and bias, and intentional attempts to manipulate through lies or half-truths. When someone flat out lies, she is stacking the deck in the most egregious way, but more often people commit fallacies or fall prey to them because they aren't paying attention to logic.

Thus, this chapter details the most common fallacies, discusses how to avoid them, and explores them through an extended example from nineteenth-century satirist, David Ross Locke.

B. Logos Fallacies

Hasty Generalization Fallacy

A hasty generalization occurs when the arguer generalizes based on a sample size that is too small or biased in some way (in other words, a sample that is not safe to generalize from). This generalization may also occur when there are statistics or numbers out of context.

> Example: Suppose you tried Greek food once; you had one dish at one restaurant. Because you didn't like this one dish, you decide, "I don't like Greek food." Or suppose you visit two news websites, you don't see a story on a subject you're looking for, and then conclude no news agencies covered the story.

What this fallacy is not: a simple or an unqualified generalization (for example, based on decades of teaching, we can say that students often think generalization and hasty generalization are the same thing). An unqualified generalization is one that implies the claim is universal, as in "Prussians were rude." A qualified generalization uses words called qualifiers to make the claim more accurate, by intensifying or clarifying, as in "All Prussian generals in the aforementioned meeting used rude words" and "Many members of the Prussian upper class were rude."

Begging the Question, or Circular Reasoning Fallacy

This fallacy occurs when an arguer's logic just goes around in a circle; instead of presenting evidence, the claim *is* the evidence. The most common example is the claim that god is real because the

Bible says so (this only works if you believe the Bible presents true facts because a real god wrote it). There are secular examples too. Think of when you might have said the following: I'm not going to watch that dumb TV show, because it's dumb. You would need to explain *why* it's dumb to be logical.

Red Herring Fallacy

The arguer mentions something irrelevant to distract the audience from the actual argument. This happens every election cycle. In fact, some issues are considered "election red herrings," meaning politicians only talk about them during election years, when they want to rile people up.

> Example: The most famous example of a red herring is the "Checkers" story. In short, a politician, Richard Nixon, had some campaign donations go missing. The press wanted to know where the money went. One of the donors had also given Nixon's family a dog, Checkers. In the press conference, Nixon held the dog up by the ears and said he shouldn't have to take his daughter's dog away because it came from a donor. This story is famous because it worked. The reporters got distracted by a dog, and the real question was dropped.

Straw Man Fallacy

This fallacy is a version of the red herring, when the arguer misrepresents the opposition view (notice that Nixon does this by implying the reporters want to take a little girl's dog away). Instead of fighting an actual opponent, the arguer sets up a straw man, meaning someone easy to knock down. Think of how often a politician says something like "my opponent wants this country to fail." Isn't it more likely that the opponent merely has different ideas about how to improve the country?

> Example: Jon Stewart pointed out another straw man fallacy when discussing George W. Bush with a biographer, Robert

Draper. In response to Bush's father and friends, who weren't certain that invading Iraq was a good idea, Bush said, "You can't talk me out of thinking freedom's a good thing." Stewart: "He's inventing arguments. This is the classic straw man. Who has ever tried to discuss freedom as not a good thing?"

Setting up straw men is *not* the way to handle counter-argument. Don't do it.

Stacking the Deck Fallacy

"Stacking the deck" is the term used when the arguer only provides evidence that supports his point or presents evidence in a biased way. Note that many authors commit this by refusing to engage with counter-argument. Contrast it with the *straw man argument*.

> Example: We are deciding where to go for dinner. I talk about all of the tasty dishes at one of the restaurants, leaving out the great food at the others. I obviously want to go to the one I'm talking up.

Non sequitur Fallacy

A non sequitur (literally, "it does not follow") fallacy occurs when an arguer makes a claim in which the logic simply doesn't work. These statements can usually be put into the "if x, then y" form.

> Example: From the *Album of the Soundtrack of the Trailer of the Film Monty Python and the Holy Grail*, in which a professor of logic discusses a character's false supposition (this is a comic piece, not an argument by a real professor):
>
> The last scene was interesting from the point of view of a professional logician because it contained a number of logical fallacies, that is, invalid propositional constructions and syllogistic forms, of the type so often committed by my wife. "All wood burns," states Sir Bedevere. "Therefore," he concludes, "all that burns is wood." This is, of course, pure

bullsh**. Universal affirmatives can only be partially con-
verted: all of Alma Cogan is dead, but only some of the class
of dead people are Alma Cogan. "Oh yes," one would think.
However, my wife does not understand this necessary limi-
tation of the conversion of a proposition; consequently, she
does not understand me, for how can a woman expect to
appreciate a professor of logic, if the simplest cloth-eared
syllogism causes her to flounder? For example, given the
premise, "all fish live under water" and "all mackerel are
fish," my wife will conclude, not that "all mackerel live
under water," but that "if she buys kippers, it will not rain,"
or that "trout live in trees," or even that I do not love her
anymore." This she calls "using her intuition." I call it crap,
and it gets me very irritated because it is not logical.

Slippery Slope Fallacy

Also called the "camel's nose fallacy," a slippery slope is a type of
non sequitur where the arguer assumes that if we allow A to happen, B and C and D, etc. will also inevitably happen. Jay Michaelson, writing at *Salon.com*, says of this fallacy, "You don't decide
the ethical value of a decision based on other decisions; you decide
based on the decision at hand. Is euthanasia of a brain-dead human
being morally permissible? Maybe or maybe not, but the answer
does not depend upon the slippery slope of whether it's permissible
in other cases, say, of chronic pain, or mere dislike of aging. The
slippery slope is a dangerous fallacy."

When Karma first went to college, she was pursuing a theater
degree. Her grandmother said that if Karma got that degree, she
would die of AIDS. The grandmother's argument was a stack of
non sequiturs (and scientific misunderstandings): if Karma got that
degree, she would be in plays; in plays, she would eventually have
to kiss an actor; all actors are gay; thus, all actors have AIDS; thus,
the kiss would kill Karma. Yes, this is a real example.[1]

---

1 Karma would like you to know that she did go ahead and get that theater
   degree, and she's still alive!

Post Hoc, Ergo Propter Hoc Fallacy

Post hoc, ergo propter hoc is Latin for "after this, therefore because of this." It's often shortened to *post hoc* and is also called false cause, coincidental correlation, or correlation without causation. A *post hoc* fallacy is when the arguer gets cause and effect wrong, usually because he has assumed that because one thing happened before another, the first thing caused the second. This fallacy causes many superstitions. It's also very common because we're trying to make sense of the world, using the information we can see. If we see x and then y happens, we assume x caused y.

> Example: Perhaps you have a headache and take a herbal supplement. Your headache goes away. Did the medicine cause your headache to go away, or was it the soda you drank with the medication (since simple caffeine can eliminate some headaches)?

Either/Or Fallacy

The arguer insists that there are only two options, and only one is right. This is also called the "false dilemma."

> Example: "You're either for us or against us."

> Example: A teacher tells you that you can either study for the quiz or fail it. There are actually many combinations of outcomes (you could study and still fail, for example).

Argument from the Negative Fallacy

This form of the false dilemma is when an arguer first says there are only two positions. She then says, "since I can prove you wrong, I'm right." This is not logical because she and her opponent can both be wrong.

> Example: Two doctors are debating a diagnosis. One doctor, with a blood test, proves that her colleague's guess is wrong.

If she then asserts that she's right, she's committed a fallacy. The patient could be suffering from a third problem that neither has considered.

Appeal to a Lack of Evidence Fallacy

An appeal to lack of evidence (*argumentum ad ignorantium*, literally "argument from ignorance") occurs when the arguer dismisses the opponent's argument because the opponent doesn't have evidence (or the kind of evidence the arguer prefers).

> Example: Think about a murder trial. The prosecutor argues that person x killed person y. The prosecutor might not have enough evidence to prove this to a jury. In this case, the prosecutor is *not convincing*, but it doesn't make him *wrong*. Person x may well be the murderer. Furthermore, note that x won't be judged innocent, just "not guilty" of this charge, in this trial.

> Example: A student was once writing a response to a courtship (dating) guide from a century and a half ago. The student said the author of the guide wasn't *right* because she didn't cite studies. One should not expect the author of such a guide to be able to find or cite scientific studies proving that men were expected to be polite to women.

Students also often accidentally commit this fallacy because they don't understand it. They might be arguing with a friend who does not have evidence, and they will claim their opponent is wrong because of the "lack of evidence" fallacy. In this case, it is the students who are committing the fallacy, not the friend. You can say your opponent isn't *convincing* if she doesn't have evidence, but you can't say she is *wrong*.

Quick Fix Fallacy

The arguer simply argues in slogans or chooses a solution that is quick and easy, but that doesn't solve the problem. Examples of the former are common in debates about gun control in the US. Phrases like "guns don't kill people, people do" and "when guns are outlawed, only outlaws will have guns" are often meant to be debate enders, although they oversimplify the debate.

> Example: For the latter kind of quick fix, one might consider Lisa Simpson's critique of a Brazilian strategy in "Blame It on Lisa."
>
> **Marge:** What a charming neighborhood.
> **Lisa:** Mom, those are slums. The government just painted them bright colors so the tourists wouldn't be offended.
> **Marge:** Works for me!

Faulty Analogy Fallacy
When the arguer compares two things, but the comparison doesn't lead to a logical conclusion.

> Example: The silliest example Karma ever heard was when a woman on TV argued that we shouldn't teach sex education in schools because "we don't just hand kids the keys to the car—we know driving, like sex, is dangerous." Not only was this a faulty analogy, her analogy was evidence *against* her point. We don't just hand kids the keys to the car. We have driver's education in schools and mandate seat belt use. By her logic, instead of the "don't have sex" education we tend to see today, we should have even *more* instructive sex education and mandate contraception.

Sunken Cost Fallacy
The arguer is reluctant to stop doing something that isn't effective, because the arguer has already spent so much time on it, money on it, etc. We often encourage students to change their topics if their current essay isn't working out; too many students say, "but I've already written two paragraphs!"

Example: We also sometimes see this when people won't leave a clearly failing relationship or when they keep spending a lot of money to fix a car that's just going to break in another way next month: "I just spent $800 fixing this car, so I'll put in another $400, because I shouldn't have to get a new one."

Whataboutism Fallacy

Whataboutism, which is the new name for the *tu quoque* fallacy, happens when the arguer, who is being criticized, deflects blame by criticizing his opponent with the same critique, saying "but what about x?" The arguer thinks he is winning by calling his opponent a hypocrite, but other people's bad behavior doesn't mean our own isn't bad. An example might be a student who is told he needs to improve his transitions by a peer reviewer and counters with "but what about your awkward transition in your last paper?" It's not a logical response to criticism.

Three Logical Fallacies Common in Literary Analysis

Biographical Fallacy

The arguer assumes the author of a piece of fiction (or poem or song, etc.) can't actually write fiction and thus that every piece is autobiographical.

Example: Margaret Atwood has had some fun with this fallacy. In her satirical essay, "Under the Thumb," she notes, "it's a feature of our times that if you write fiction, everyone assumes that the people and events in it are disguised biography—but if you write your biography, it's assumed you're lying your head off." Atwood should know; readers frequently make this assumption about her novels, as is clear in the following example. After publishing a novel in which a character gained a lot of weight, readers kept asking Atwood how she lost weight, assuming the character was biographical. Atwood noted, in a public lecture that Karma attended, that she writes male characters all the time, but that no one asks her when she lost her penis.

Intentional Fallacy

The arguer assumes that she knows what was in a writer's mind when he wrote his piece (i.e., she knows what he intended).

Example: Many readers argued that Octavia Butler *intended* her story, "Bloodchild," (which was about how desperate human settlers on an alien world were required to participate in alien gestation to be allowed to stay) to be read as a metaphor for slavery. She was surprised by that reading, however, as she later explained in an essay.

The Reception Fallacy

Karma identified and named this one; it led to her dissertation. It's when a reader or viewer states (without evidence) that the entire audience of a text reacted the same way. An example might be when a student says, "readers were confused by the change in point of view," when in fact the rest of the class understood the changes perfectly. This might be considered a form a hasty generalization; the author's sample size is just herself.

Example: Often, Karma has her health science students compare and contrast Mary Roach's and Atul Gawande's writing styles. Some students assert that the audience trusts Gawande more because he's a doctor. There is no evidence for this; the student is generalizing from her own reaction to the text. Thus, the student should say, "I find myself giving more trust to Gawande" or "since Gawande is a doctor, audiences may trust him more." Those are both true statements, and are therefore safe to include in an evaluation.

C. Pathos Fallacies

Ad Hominem Fallacy

With the *ad hominem* fallacy, the arguer attacks the opponent's character instead of engaging in a logical argument. This is called mudslinging, and you see it all the time during elections. What this is *not*: attacking your opponent's *argument* or evidence. Those are fair game, if you're logical and unbiased.

> Example: We are debating your idea for how to format a PowerPoint slide. I argue that we can't use your idea because you wet the bed until you were 11.

Some believe that you should *never* attack character, but certain arguers invite you to. These are arguers who say, "trust me, I'm moral" or "I'm the family values candidate." If you're going to take the moral high ground, make sure you actually have it. In other words, if you *ask* us to judge you on your character, we will.

Ad Populum Fallacy

The *ad populum* fallacy occurs when the writer appeals plainly to emotion rather than logic. This is misused pathos. We see this any time someone talks about "innocent children." Any statement combined with "innocent children" is just going for your gut. (The arguer is hoping you don't say, "as opposed to the *guilty* children?")

There are many basic *ad populum* approaches:

- *Peer Pressure* (other people will call this bandwagon, even though we don't have bandwagons anymore): everybody's doing it.
- *Patriotic Appeal*: also called draping oneself in the flag; asserting that people who disagree with you are disloyal.
- *Religious Appeal*: saying that your way is right because it fits your interpretation of God, of morality, of values. You are

implying that those who disagree with you disagree with God and are thus amoral or immoral.

- *Snob Appeal*: rather than asserting that everybody's doing it, you assert, "the *best* people are doing it."
- *Plain Folks*: the arguer explains that he or his position is superior because he's just a regular person. Often, the "regular" guy is implying that it's better to be less educated than to be an egghead, better to be from the heartland than to be city folks, better to be inexperienced than to be a career politician, etc. Anti-intellectualism is usually part of this appeal. Some might consider this to be the opposite of the snob approach, but the two appeals share a commonality: they both appeal to our desires to be "insiders," to belong to a desired group or tribe.
- *Appeal to the Majority*: asserting that you're right because most people agree with you. As we know, most people can be wrong. At one time, most people thought the sun revolved around the Earth, after all.

Appeal to Tradition Fallacy

The arguer believes an activity or belief is valid because it's been a "tradition." This is most commonly seen with holidays and other festivals. Why does the father walk a bride down the aisle? Tradition. Why do people put wreaths on the door at Christmas time? Tradition. Both of these traditions came from somewhere; most people don't know what they symbolize anymore. We're not arguing that you can't follow traditions, by the way, just know that's an emotional reason, not a logical one.

Hypostatization Fallacy

In this subset of appeal to tradition, the arguer refers to traditional belief in vague terms, giving no specific evidence ("history has taught us…" or "science has proven…").

Appeal to Novelty Fallacy
This is the opposite of the appeal to tradition. Here, you argue that if something's older or the traditional way to do it, it must be replaced with the newer option.

Appeal to Age Fallacy
Similar to the appeal to tradition, this is when we are asked to defer to age, as if age is always accompanied by wisdom or knowledge. While our grandparents may have had some good ideas, they also had some bad ones. We have to sort out which are which.

Appeal to Youth Fallacy
This is the opposite of the appeal to age. Not surprisingly, this is often committed by the younger generation, who think their ways of doing things are best.

> Example: Karma's students often argue that they're actually more intelligent than previous generations because they have easier access to more information than previous generations, but then they email her to ask where her office building is located. Karma shakes her head (she had to figure out those things with paper maps). In addition, she knows that if a student is on a device that can email her, it could also Google "Voorhies Hall."

D. Ethos Fallacy

Appeal to Improper or Biased Authority Fallacy
An appeal to improper or biased authority happens when the arguer believes someone simply because she's a celebrity. But a celebrity might not know which brand of popcorn pops best and may not give you all the facts, because she is paid to advertise and therefore has something to gain.

Example: A mechanic may tell you that parts of your car need to be replaced. This could be his expert opinion or because he needs to make money.

Note that *appealing to authority* is fine (in fact, it's one of the ways we build ethos—borrowing other people's), as long as that authority is not improper or biased.

E. Avoiding Fallacies

Note that there are additional problems with logic that you will see. Writers may exaggerate the importance of an issue, they may exaggerate their evidence, they may tamper with evidence, or they may lie outright.

It's vital to know about logical fallacies so you can avoid being manipulated by them. You should also be aware that you probably commit these, perhaps unintentionally, as well. To be an ethical arguer, you shouldn't.

Here are some ways to avoid them.

- Don't generalize without evidence. This can help you avoid the hasty generalization and the reception fallacy. Don't say "the audience" when you mean "me" or "me and my friends" or "the audience in the Varsity theater on 5/3/18."
- Ask yourself if you're being fair:
  - Do I understand the opposition viewpoint, or am I making assumptions about it?
  - Have I given my audience all the information they need to decide, or have I just told them about my side?
  - Have I unintentionally exaggerated?
  - Have I unintentionally implied that there are only two choices?

Sometimes, we end up saying something fallacious because we honestly don't know any better. This is why we must pay attention to our word choice and phrasing. When in doubt, look up terms, especially when you're new to a field. For example, many students say Shakespearean English is "Old English." It's actually "Early Modern English." Old English is from centuries before; it's basically a foreign language, requiring a lot of training to understand (we can't read Old English, even though we have PhDs in Literature!).

To avoid lying, really think about what you're saying. Many of our students have proposed such falsehoods as "everyone today relies on GPS instead of paper maps." Well, not Amish people or people hiking outside of cellphone service range. You might think you'd get lost all the time if GPS didn't exist, but you'd probably figure out how to use a map.

Be honest in your phrasing. Usually, when we state an opinion, we don't need to mark it with an "I." For example, if we say, "boiled asparagus is gross," you know it's an opinion. However, we sometimes need to be clearer when we give an opinion that might be mistaken as a fact.

Example:
Possibly mistaken as fact: "The movie was confusing."

Was it inherently confusing or were *you* confused? There is a difference, and you need to be clear.

Honest: "Since I was texting my mom during the movie, I couldn't follow the plot."
Honest: "Because the director didn't signal the flashbacks, some audience members may not have realized we were jumping back 20 years in scene two."

You can also be honest by not generalizing, by using *some, many, may,* etc. Avoid words like *proves, definitely, obviously,* etc. As we mentioned in Chapter One, these words are called qualifiers.[2]

Once, Karma gave students an assignment to find a journal article in their field and to analyze it. They had to identify the citation style, which they could do from going to the journal website to see what they wanted submissions to be formatted in. One student wrote: "The citation style is not clear."

That just wasn't true.

One is not allowed to publish an article without following a citation style correctly. The student couldn't identify the style because the student didn't follow the instructions on how to figure it out, but note that the student's use of passive voice implies that the *published author made a mistake.* That's a lie.

F. Locke's Lesson in Logic

In 1868, American satirist David Ross Locke gave a speech on "the woman question." People at the time were debating the issues raised by the first-wave feminist movement, in which women (and men!) argued for women's right to vote, to work, and to be paid enough to support themselves.

Arguments against the feminist movement included assertions that women were naturally meant to only be wives and mothers and that women must be ruled by men because Eve tasted the apple first in the Old Testament story.

We love Locke's answer to these and other objections, but his speech is incredibly long, so we have condensed it. The audience

2 Qualifiers are simple little words, but they make a huge difference. Look at how Weird Al used them for comic effect in his almost-love song, "Good Enough for Now": "Now it seems to me I'm relatively lucky / I know I probably couldn't ask for too much more / I honestly can say you're an above-average lady / You're almost just what I've been looking for."

would have understood that the views below belong to Locke's satiric persona, not to the real Locke.

I adore woman, but I want her to keep her place. In our higher walks of life, she is a toy to be played with and is bought and sold; in the lower strata, she bears the burdens and does the drudgery of servants. But I am sure that her present condition is her proper condition, for it has always been so.

Man, it will be observed, was created first, showing conclusively that he was intended to take precedence of woman. A schoolmistress of mine once denied the correctness of this conclusion. "If there is anything in being first," she said, "man must acknowledge the supremacy of the goose, for according to Genesis, the fowl was first created."

Such an argument, of course, I reject with scorn.

I find in the Bible many arguments against the equality of woman with man in point of intellectual power. The serpent tempted Eve, not Adam. Why did he select Eve? Ah, why, indeed!

Satan selected Eve because the woman was weaker than the man, and therefore best for his purpose.

At this point, however, we must stop. Should we go on, we would find that Eve, the weak woman, tempted Adam, the strong man, with distinguished success, which would leave us in this predicament: Satan, stronger than Eve, tempted her to indulge in fruit. Eve's weakness was demonstrated by her falling a victim to temptation. Eve tempted Adam; Adam yielded to Eve; therefore—but I shall dismiss Adam and Eve with the remark that if Satan had been considerate of the feelings of the conservatives, his best friends, by the way, in all ages, he would have tempted Adam first and caused Adam to tempt Eve.

The disturbing female, my former schoolmistress, maintains that women's qualifications entitle them to vote. I answer that such is not the case. For example, my friend is learned. She has read the Constitution of the United States. She excels in political lore the great majority of our representatives in Congress. Nevertheless, I protest against her voting for several reasons:

1. She cannot sing bass. Her voice is pitched higher than the male voice, which indicates feminine weakness of mind.

2. Her form is graceful rather than strong.

3. She delights in millinery goods.[3]

4. She can't grow whiskers.

In all of these points, nature has made a distinction between the sexes [that] cannot be overlooked.

Let every woman marry and marry as soon as possible. Then she is provided for. Then, if her husband is a good man, a kind man, an honest man, a sober man, an industrious man, and if he has a good business and drives it, and meets with no misfortunes, and never yields to temptations, why, then, the maid promoted to be his wife will be tolerably certain to, at least, have all that she can eat, and all that she can wear, as long as he continues so.

However, this strange woman, of whom I have spoken, remarked that she wanted women to have an opportunity to stand alone in case she could not marry or her husband proved incompetent to support her. She demanded for woman, in short, employment at anything she was capable of doing, and pay precisely the same that men receive for the same labor provided she does it as well.

This is a clear flying in the face of Providence. It is utterly impossible that any woman can do any work as well as men. Nature decreed it otherwise. Ask the clerks at Washington, whose muscular frames are employed at the arduous and exhausting labor of writing in books and counting money, and cutting out extracts from newspapers, and endorsing papers and filing them, what they think of that?

---

3 That means she likes hats.

I asked her sternly, "Are you willing to go to war? Did you shoulder a musket in the late unpleasantness [the American Civil War]?"

She merely asked me if I carried a musket in the late war? Certainly I did not. I had too much presence of mind to volunteer. Nor did the majority of those holding official position. But there is this difference: We *could* have gone while women could not. And it is better that it is so. In the event of another bloody war, one so desperate as to require all the patriotism of the country to show itself, I do not want my wife to go to the tented field, even though she have the requisite physical strength. No, indeed! I want her to stay at home—with me.

In the matter of wages, I do not see how it is to be helped. The woman who teaches receives, if she has thoroughly mastered the requirements of the position, say, six hundred dollars a year, while a man occupying the same position, filling it with equal ability, receives twice that amount, and possibly three times. But what is this to me? As a man of business, my duty to myself is to get my children educated at the least possible expense. As there are very few things women are permitted to do, and as, for every vacant place, there are a hundred women eager for it, their pay—as a matter of course—is brought down to a fine point.

There are immutable laws governing all these things—the laws of supply and demand. Christ, whose mission was with the poor, made other laws, but Christ is not allowed to have anything to do with business. Selfishness is older than Christ, and we conservatives stick close to the oldest.

As I said some minutes ago, if the men born into the world would marry at twenty-one, each a maiden of eighteen, and take care of her properly, and never get drunk or sick, or anything of that inconvenient sort, and both would be taken at precisely the same time with consumption, yellow fever, cholera or any of those ailments, and employ the same physician, that they might go out of the world at the same moment, it would be well. The men would then take care of the women.

Women are themselves to blame for a great part of the distress they experience. There is work for them, if they would only do it. The kitchens of the country are not half supplied with intelligent labor, and therein is a refuge for all women in distress. I assert that nothing but foolish pride, which is sinful, keeps the daughters and widows of insolvency out of kitchens, where they may have happy underground homes and three dollars per week, by merely doing six hours per day more labor than [construction workers] average.

But women will not all submit. Refusing to acknowledge the position in life nature fixed for them, they rebel, and unpleasantness takes place. An incident [that] fell under my observation recently beautifully illustrates this.

A young lady, named Jane Evans, I believe, had sustained the loss of both her parents. Jane purchased some needles, and renting a room in the uppermost part of a building in a secluded section of New York, commenced a playful effort to live by making shirts, at eighteen cents each. She was situated, I need not say, pleasantly for one of her class. Her room was not large, it is true, but as she had no cooking stove or bedstead, what did she want of a large room? She had a window, which did not open, but as there was no glass in it, she had no occasion to open it. This building commanded a beautiful view of the back parts of other buildings similar in appearance, and the sash kept out a portion of the smell. In this delightful retreat, she sat and sat and sewed and sewed. Sometimes, in her zeal, she would sew till late in the night, and she was always at her work very early in the morning. She paid rent promptly, for the genial old gentleman of whom she leased her room had a sportive habit of kicking girls into the street who did not pay promptly. She managed every now and then, did this economical girl, to purchase a loaf of bread, which she ate.

One Saturday night, she took her bundle of work to the delightful man who employed her. Her employer found fault with the making of these shirts. "They are not properly sewed," he said, and he could not, in consequence, pay her. Jane then, injudiciously cried about it, and her employer who was, and is, possessed of a tender heart, and cannot bear to see a woman cry, kicked her out of his store into the snow.

What did this wicked girl do? Did she go back and ask pardon of her good, tender-hearted employer? Not she! On the contrary, she clenched her hands, and, passing by a baker's shop, stole a loaf of bread, and, brazen thing that she was, she ate it in front of the shop! She said she was hungry, though it was subsequently proven that she had eaten within forty-eight hours. She was arraigned for petty larceny and sent to jail for sixty days.

Now, see how surely evildoers come to bad ends. The wretched Jane—this fearfully depraved Jane—unable, after such a manifestation of depravity, to hold up her head, fell into bad ways. Remorse for the stealing of that loaf of bread so preyed upon her, that she wandered about the streets of New York for five days, asking for work, and finally threw herself off a wharf.

So you see demonstrated the mischief that comes from women attempting to move out from their sphere. Women who do not want to steal bread, and be arrested, and go off wharves, must take pay as it is offered, whether they get anything to eat or not. Had this wretched girl gone back contentedly to her room, and starved to death cheerfully, she would not have stolen bread, and would have saved the City of New York the expense and trouble of fishing her out of the East River.

Alas! Such women always make trouble.

Locke's use of the word "conservative" here means someone who values tradition and resists change. Thus, his persona uses the tradition fallacy to justify the continued mistreatment of women. Most of his assertions, however, are actually non sequiturs.

Satires often feature naïve narrators, who can't see their lack of logic. Locke also shows that his persona's arguments can't withstand the schoolteacher's scrutiny. Another tactic in satire is to extend the opposing side's logic—a logical argument should still be logical when applied to similar circumstances. But man's supremacy falls apart if it's just based on which sex was made first. And Locke's persona acknowledges that by conservative logic, Eve is actually morally stronger than Adam.[4]

Locke also points out that the way some conservatives argue society *should* work is not actually practical. As his long list of "if"s makes clear, a woman's ability to be taken care of just by being married makes her health and safety precarious. The speech's audience would have understood how impossible it would be to guarantee that any given man would be perfect, especially in a time of rampant alcoholism. The fight for the right to vote was often also supported by people who wanted to ban alcohol, due to its destructive effects on family life. The 1800s are famous as the time when Americans drank the most. If a woman's husband couldn't keep a job due to drinking or used all the family income on alcohol, she wouldn't be able to divorce him or to take a job with equivalent pay.

Many unmarried women also needed to support themselves, and while Locke's persona disparages Jane Evans, we are meant to feel for her and to condemn the unfairness of her situation.

Finally, Locke's essay showcases a perennial source of humor for satirists and comedians—clever attacks on government representatives of all parties. It's not surprising, then, that Locke has been referred to as the Stephen Colbert of the Civil War era (Grinspan).

---

4 Karma wishes she could go back in time and show this part to her younger self, who heard this very old argument about Eve being weaker, in church.

CHAPTER FIVE

The Search
The Research Process

A. Introduction

B. Why Your Librarian Is Better Than Google (Scholar)

C. How to Find Academic Sources

D. How to Find Non-academic Sources

E. Notes on Notes

A. Introduction

This is the most common mistake young scholars make in their research:

Say a professor says students need a minimum of three sources. The student then stops the research process at the first three sources she finds.

Are all three of the sources relevant to the topic? Do they just repeat the same information? Do they all simply agree with the student's thesis? Are there more relevant sources? Has she found enough information to back up her points? Has she found authors' works that will provide background on the topic? Has she found authors who disagree with her ideas, so she can engage with counter-argument effectively? Are these sources reliable? Might there be a benefit to doing more than the minimum required for a C? Maybe she doesn't care.

Dear reader, we hope you care.

Now that you know how to evaluate sources, this chapter will help you find them.

But first, two cautionary notes:

First, most young scholars do their research in the wrong order. Imagine a professor in a PoliSci class asks you to write a paper on whether the UN should acknowledge Palestine as an independent country. Many people will mistakenly pick a position and then do research to back it up. That's not how we do research in the real world. Instead, we start with a question, and perhaps a hypothesis, but the research is what leads us to our answer, our conclusion, our argument, our thesis.

One of the problems with doing the research after you have your answer or thesis is that you will only seek out research that agrees with you, resulting in incomplete ideas and an unconvincing argument.

Imagine how this backwards order of research could taint arguments. A food critic reviews a new restaurant. He is supposed to go in with an open mind, right? His research, eating there, should determine his answer. Only a very bad (and unreliable) critic would cherry-pick his experience to fit his preconceived thesis and decide to give the restaurant 4/5 stars, no matter how the food tasted, no matter how the service was, and no matter how dirty the bathroom was.

If we think about this from a scientific standpoint, we know that we can't start with the answer. All research, all experiments, start with questions. A scientific team might ask themselves: Is x heart medicine more effective for women who have had heart attacks than y medicine? They might look at some of the literature out there about the drugs to formulate their hypothesis—that y is better. Then they have to do a lot more research. When they're conducting the research, they can't overlook evidence that x is better (fewer side effects, perhaps).

They have to be willing to change their minds—to let the research decide the truth.

Moreover, even if their hypothesis is disproven by their research—they have still learned something and thus added to their field of knowledge. We needed to know that y isn't better, whether their experiment showed that x is more effective or that the drugs are really pretty much the same.

Atul Gawande, in his book, *Better*, has a chapter about how the American Medical Association (AMA) doesn't allow physicians to assist in executions in America. Gawande explains that he started his research as someone who was pro-death penalty. In trying to figure out whether the AMA should change their guidelines, he found that he could never be the physician in the room at an execution, because he would violate his Hippocratic Oath by intentionally doing harm. His research not only led him to agree with the AMA, but to change his mind on the death penalty.

Second, if you do your research correctly, you will find more sources than you could ever use in your argument. Some will turn out to be tangential to your argument. Others will just repeat the same points. Only use and cite what you need. We expect that you read more than you cited. (If you really really really want to "show your work," you can add a works consulted list after your works cited list.)

B. Why Your Librarian Is Better Than Google (Scholar)

Once, a student in a Health Science Writing class asked Karma if he had to come to the next session that was with their Health Science Librarian. "I mean, she's just going to show us Google, right? I know how to use that."

Karma assured the student that he definitely had to come to the next session. She explained that if he thought the beginning and end of research could be found with Google, then he needed the session a lot. During that class, he was furiously taking notes; he had no idea about how medical professionals do research.

Ruth Gustafson, our Health Science Librarian, often uses this metaphor when talking to our students: as they are entering the profession, they want to use precision tools for their work and their research. They want a lancet to take blood, not a butter knife.

Google is the butter knife.

Chapter Three discussed the problems with Google, so we won't repeat them here. However, note that Google Scholar, even with better results, has significant drawbacks. As Chapter Two explains, not all "peer-reviewed" open-source journals are actually reliable, but you can access them on Google, and thus accidentally use bad research to back up your own. When you are on the trail of a good article on Google, you might hit a pay wall.

If you start with your university or college library, you will never hit a pay wall. Whether we find a book or an article, if our university doesn't have it, we can hit a button that says "request," and the book will show up in a couple of days in our library for us to pick up. The article will be scanned by another library and show up in our email in-box.

As long as we start our research before the last minute, we can get what we need.

In this chapter, we will talk about how to search your library for good sources, but the superior scholar won't just do all the work from her laptop; she will also have a meeting (or a few) with her subject librarian.

Subject librarians usually have degrees and/or work experience in their field. They also have a Masters in Library Science. That's a whole degree in finding and evaluating information. We don't have that degree, which is why we use our subject librarians.

Subject librarians are the people who decide what books the library will buy, what journals and databases the library will subscribe to. They know how to use unique database search terms to find exactly what they need. They can help you narrow down your topic and decide what kind of essay you need to write to answer your research question.

They also love helping polite students find what they need. Once, one of Karma's students was having trouble finding out how much anti-rattlesnake venom for dogs was available in the US. Ruth found out within the day.

C. How to Find Academic Sources

Although you should definitely consult with your subject librarian, you still need to know how to find academic sources on your own. To search and cite correctly, you need to understand basic genre terms and the flow of publication. In other words, you have to be able to tell the difference between a novel, an editorial in a newspaper, and a peer-reviewed article. We hope you just said to yourself, "well, duh," but we have to say that students misidentify genres all the time. According to them, Shakespeare writes novels, authors have their works published in databases, and there's no difference between a book by a single author and an edited collection.

Part of understanding genre is understanding the publication flow. An author writes a text—a book, a letter to the editor, a chapter in an edited collection, a research article, etc. A publisher publishes the book; the newspaper prints the letter (or posts it in the online edition); a publisher prints the edited collection, after the editor compiles and edits all of the chapters; a publisher publishes the academic journal the research article will appear in, etc.

Academic databases then index all the books and journals in a particular field. (Sometimes newspapers and magazines are included in these databases, but there are databases just for news too.) The databases pay to have access to these resources. Your university library then pays to have the physical and electronic books, some journals, and the major databases their students, faculty, and staff will need.

When a scholar is starting out, she doesn't know what books are out there, she doesn't know what the major journals are in her field, and she probably doesn't know which database indexes are the best for her to use.

So where does she start?

With her library's subject guides.

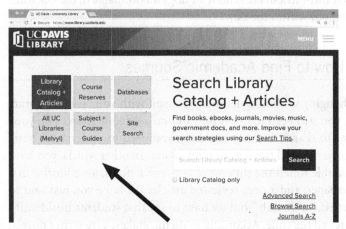

Figure 5.1 A screenshot of the UC Davis main library page. Notice the subject guide link is prominently featured.

Figure 5.2 A screenshot of the Los Rios Community College District Library Research Databases page, which starts with general searches. Note the links on the side for subject guides (one could also reach these by scrolling down).

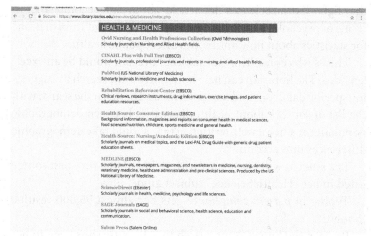

Figure 5.3 A screenshot of the Los Rios Community College District Library Research Databases page. Here, we've scrolled down to the Health and Medicine Subject Guide.

To use the full resources of your library, you need to be logged on. At our university, if you're on a school computer, you can always get into our material. However, if you're on your phone or laptop at home or wherever, you have to log in through the VPN; otherwise, the library assumes you're just a member of the public, and you won't have access to free articles and resources.

When we go to our library's subject guide list, we essentially see a list of majors that our university offers. However, don't limit your search to your major. You need to think about where the information you need might be.

Say a student is writing on problems with patient compliance, regarding finishing antibiotics. She should probably start with the "Health Science" subject guide, but she should also consider "Biological Science" if she needs resources about antibiotics and what they fight, "Social Sciences" for articles about patient compliance in terms of psychology or sociology, and "Government Information" for statistics about how antibiotics affect public health.

This is why consulting her subject librarian would be an excellent idea. The librarian can help both narrow the search by suggesting specific databases and search terms and broaden the search with the list of sources about health disparities between demographic populations, since a well-written article should take demographic differences into account.

The student will likely start with PubMed, the very first source listed in her "Health Science" subject guide.

Typing in *patient compliance* gets her almost 95,000 results, though.

Perhaps she knows some search tips, because she's been to her university's library orientation or met with her librarian.

Therefore, she knows to put "patient compliance" into quotation marks if the words need to be right next to each other in the search. She knows if she then puts AND (in all caps) and antibiotic*, she will be searching for both of those terms in the same work. The asterisk means that the database will search for *antibiotic* and *antibiotics*. Now she only has 1,000 results. She can further narrow down by language, by year, by species, by sex of the patient, by age of patient, and by text availability (in other words, she could narrow down to only articles she could read right away, though she shouldn't, since her library could get her anything she needs in just a couple of days).

In scrolling through her results, she sees a study from China, finding that out of over 700 patients, about 87 per cent weren't fully compliant. The abstract also tells her that the researchers found many demographic impacts on who was more likely to be compliant. From reading the abstract, she might decide to read the whole article, or she may decide that she wants to focus on Western compliance in her essay. However, she should take a look at the Chinese study's list of works cited. These researchers had to research this, so they have done a lot of work for her. She can trace their research back to useful articles for herself. She should also look at the search terms this article is indexed under in the database, discovering that "antibacterial" is another word she might want to add (with an OR) after antibiotic*.

If she really wants to dig into PubMed, she'll have the librarian show her how to dig into the PubMed MESH. She might then go into Embase, another database in her subject guide that looks promising, where she finds that "patient complian*" AND antibiotic* yields over 5,600 results. (She figured out, based on Embase's text prediction, that patient compliance might be listed under patient compliant, and thus added the asterisk.) In addition to narrowing down all the ways she could in PubMed, she can now narrow by drug name, by the kind of study (an actual trial with human tissue, a meta-study,...), etc.

If she's logged in via her library, not only can she immediately see some articles and request others, but she can email her search results to herself. She can save her searches to come back to them later. If she's in grad school or doing a more in-depth project, she can set these databases to send her notifications when new sources on her topic are indexed.

Just as she should look at the works cited listings of other researchers and figure out what search terms her databases use, if she finds a book that looks promising, she should go to the shelf it's on in her library—every scholar we know has a story of finding the perfect book *next* to the book he went into the library for.

As she works, she has to carefully note what kind of source she's reading, so she can evaluate it, properly cite it, and follow her professor's instructions. For example, if her professor has said she has to find peer-reviewed articles, she needs to narrow for that. She also needs to use her genre knowledge. Not every piece in a peer-reviewed journal is a peer-reviewed article.

As we noted in Chapter Two, Karma is the editor of *Margaret Atwood Studies*, a peer-reviewed journal. This journal often has several pieces that aren't peer-reviewed: Karma's letter from the editor, introducing the issue; book reviews of books on or by

Atwood; and essays by undergraduates who won a competition the Atwood Society holds every year.

Thus, as we've stressed in Chapter One, we have to understand the context and telos of what we read, even in peer-reviewed journals.

You don't want to do what one of Karma's students did a few years ago, after Karma required that students analyze a peer-reviewed article that related to the essay they were writing. One of her students had to do the whole project over again after turning in a three-page analysis of the following "article" by Alice A. Leeds. While it's impressive that the student wrote three pages about four paragraphs, this is obviously not a peer-reviewed article; it's a letter to the editor of the journal, objecting to a point a previously published article had made.

Letters

Ages of Experimental Animals

I was agreeably impressed by Calloway's suggestion (31 Dec., p. 1771) that experimental animals should be of known ages and of different ages. Inspired to follow further his ideal of exponentially related ages, I have been planning experiments. Starting with an animal of unit age 1 year, A, I added animals, as specified by Calloway, of ages "A², A⁴, A⁸, and so on," but to my distress all seemed to be of the same ages. So I tried an animal of unit age 1/2 year, and found that my other animals were aged 1/4 year, 1/8 year, 1/16 year, and so on. This did not seem quite right, so I decided to specify my ½-year-old as aged 182½ days. Then I found that my second animal would be aged over 90 years, which seemed to limit the choice of species. It turned out that my fourth animal should be something over 3 million years old, and this is too much to cope with even for a paleontologist.

GEORGE GAYLORD SIMPSON
Museum of Comparative Zoology,
Harvard University,
Cambridge, Massachusetts

Education: The European System

I take exception to James Brian Quinn's statement ("National planning of science and technology in France," 19 Nov., p. 993) about what he refers to as "anachronistic rigidities" in the French educational system. [Quinn wrote, "Once started on an educational 'track' in childhood, a person finds it almost impossible to change to another. . . . Thus many 'late bloomers' and people who want to change careers are lost to science, engineering, and other professions."]

Having been educated in the primary, secondary, and university system of Western Europe, I believe that there are a number of advantages to the so-called track system that begins during early schooling. To understand why is it possible to make a choice between a humanistic and a science track before entering high school, one must know what the curriculum consists of before this decision is made. In the European system that I am familiar with, each student has seven or eight 45-minute periods a day. These include native language and literature, mathematics, biology, chemistry, physics, history, in short, the entire spectrum, which all students are required to take. Every year or second year a foreign language is added. Thus a student has all through grade school at least four hours each week of each subject. Before entering high school a decision is made by the student, in consultation with his parents and teachers, whether to enter a humanistically oriented (gymnasium) or a science-oriented high school. The decision is not difficult. Since he has already had nine years of history, languages, mathematics, and the natural and physical sciences, it has become quite evident where his talents lie and where his interests are strongest. Once he enters the type of high school he prefers, he still continues with some subjects of the alternate curriculum, but the stress is on his chosen general area.

Thus when one enters the university at 18 years of age to study medicine, for example, one has had the following training: 11 years of biology, mathematics (including calculus and differential equations), physics, chemistry (organic, inorganic, and analytical), geography, and study of one's native language; 9 or 10 years each of three other modern languages; 3 years each of Latin and Greek; approximately 5 years each of philosophy, history, art, industrial arts or home economics; and so forth. In the university one immediately embarks on a comprehensive preclinical curriculum of five semesters (or trimesters) followed by six semesters of clinical studies. The advantage is that one graduates from the university at 24 and earns a medical degree, which includes a lengthy thesis and oral examination, at 25 years of age. One is ready then to hang out one's shingle as a general practitioner. To become a specialist in a chosen area requires four more years of research and clinical activities.

I doubt that the free choice of subjects during the early years of schooling has given students in the United States a greater knowledge of languages or the sciences in a shorter period of time or, as a matter of fact, in any amount of time. There is some doubt in my mind that a student who has shown little or no inclination for or ability in the sciences in 9 years will suddenly feel a "calling" for a scientific career. A more intensive curriculum, which includes various subjects for long periods of time (instead of 2 years of French or mathematics, for example), will prepare the student better for an earlier decision as to his direction and will give him a more solid base of knowledge for whatever he may choose as his life career. It is my belief that the number of years and the cost of higher education in the United States could be cut considerably if the lower schools put less emphasis on options and more on a solid academic education.

ALICE A. LEEDS
7311 Spring Lake Drive,
Bethesda, Maryland

Scientific Manpower Commission and the Draft

Elinor Langer's article "Viet-Nam: Growing War and Campus Protests Threaten Student Deferments" (News and Comment, 17 Dec., p. 1567) presents a misleading picture of the policy of the Scientific Manpower Commission in helping to obtain student deferments, and implies erroneously that the SMC, in implementing that policy, has much in common with activist student groups.

The Selective Service defers fulltime students in good standing in the belief that education is a process necessary to the development of personnel for the many demands of our complex society. This procedure is an attempt to utilize the most important resource of the nation in the most effective way possible. The Scientific Manpower Commission subscribes to this belief; makes every effort to see that the regulations for student deferment and the reasons behind these regulations are known to students and universities; and attempts to help individual students or their universities in seeking review of classifica-

4 FEBRUARY 1966   517

Figure 5.4 Letter from Alice A. Leeds

Here's a quick recap of how to find academic sources:

- Talk to your librarian at various stages in your research.
- In your own searching, start with the subject guides (make a list of ones you want to check).
- Choose the databases you want to use from those subject guides.
- When in the database, narrow down to the best search terms.
- Narrow down by language, year, and type of source, if appropriate.
- Figure out which search terms the databases use and refine your search.
- Save your list of possible articles or email them to yourself.
- Request sources your library doesn't have on hand.
- When you find a good article, go into its citations to find more.

Finally, sometimes you need a physical book, perhaps because your professor has asked for that. (This is your professor's way of making sure you actually go to the library at least once.)

This is the one time when you would start with your library's main search page instead of the subject guides. Even then, you'll have to narrow down. "Patient compliance" in quotes on our library's main page yields more than 72,000 results. If we ask that it show us a book, however, we see that our campus libraries have over 400. By clicking on any of the titles, the library page will tell us more information about the book, including whether it's checked out and what its call number is. Our libraries, since they have large collections, all use the Library of Congress call numbers. With that number, we could walk into any large library in our country[1] and get that book off the shelf. Call numbers start with letters; that first letter will tell you which floor of the library to start on, since the floors are organized by call number.

If the book is checked out, we can hit "request" and the person who currently has the book will have to bring it back in a few days

---

1   Many large libraries around the world use the Library of Congress call numbers (or versions of them). Small libraries, like K–12 school libraries, often use the Dewey Decimal System.

so we can see it. If the book is at another library, we can ask that it be brought to our library, and it will be.

D. How to Find Non-academic Sources

Sometimes, we need non-academic sources, which is why we have a whole chapter in this book on evaluating them. But how do we *find* them?

- Well, there's Google, for all of its problems.

For non-academic sources, you want to avoid Google Scholar too. As with your library search, narrow your search terms so you don't get overwhelmed. You will also probably have to move past the first page, since the first page notoriously only has the most general information.

- Get thee to the library!

The library isn't just for academic sources. As we mentioned previously, there are databases just for newspapers and magazines, such as Access World News and Historic US Newspaper Indexes.

The library also has many kinds of sources for you.

If a student is writing on *Macbeth*, he can find a lot in the library. Our library brings back over 80,000 results for that search word in the library's main search page (which, remember, is NOT where he would want to start if he's looking for academic resources). The student will want to narrow down and sort through what there is. There are many copies of the play, of course. There are books and sections of books about *Macbeth*. Most are academic, but some aren't (the graphic novel adaptation of *Macbeth*, for example). If he's looking to compare adaptations, there are tons. There are peer-reviewed articles in journals the library subscribes to—again, not useful if he's looking for non-academic sources. If he narrows by the type of source, though, he discovers almost 700 audio-visual sources (movie adaptations, *Macbeth* opera albums, videos about training for the fight scenes in the play, etc.). There are thousands of newspaper articles and hundreds of pictures. There are also many patents, by a person with the last name Macbeth, which is why the student wants to make sure *Macbeth* is the subject, not the author, when searching. The student will quickly realize he needs to narrow down. Perhaps he wants to write about the misunderstood Lady Macbeth because, after reading the play, he sees that she isn't the one who first comes up with the idea to murder Duncan, even though he's seen some popular culture parodies of *Macbeth* where she is the main villain.

Remember, too, that the library gives you access to government information and special collections.

- Look for radio, video, and podcasts.

Good news sources in these formats will be the most reliable. National Public Radio (NPR) has excellent reporting, and all of it is archived on its site. There are also regional affiliates you could look at. If you were researching California wildfires, you would want to see how the local NPR station was reporting it. If you were looking at famous US Supreme Court cases, you would want to listen to the *More Perfect* podcasts about them. The BBC World News and the CBC are the British and Canadian equivalents, respectively.

Be careful, though. Each of those stations has comedy shows. The CBC's *This Is That*, which was a satire news show, should not be mistaken for real news, for example.

- Find surveys and interviews.

Or conduct your own; our next chapter tells you how to.

- Talk to people about what you're working on.

Seriously, tell your friends.

When one of our students was working on an essay about chronic pain, Karma was able to tell her about a very recent podcast she'd heard with interviews with chronic pain patients.

When Karma was doing her senior high school project, one of her doctors went out back to the dumpster to retrieve a newspaper she had just thrown away with an article that touched on Karma's topic. (In the days before the internet, we had to dig through trash sometimes. Be thankful you're doing research in the twenty-first century.)

Your friend's grandmother might be someone you can interview for your essay on Japanese American internment camps; your friend could tell you that there's a primary source ripe for the picking if you tell him what you're working on.

E. Notes on Notes

Whatever kind of note taking you do, consider the following three points.

- Be thorough and specific with your notes. Every writer has been a little sloppy at one point, trusting her memory when she shouldn't. She reads a great book, makes notes of the quotes she wants to use and what page numbers they came from. She doesn't write down the author's name, though. How could she forget that?

   She can and will, and she doesn't want to recall all the books she looked at from the library again to find that quote on that page number. However, she'll have to, if she hasn't been careful.

- In your note taking and writing, be very careful about distinguishing between quotes, summaries, paraphrases, and your own thoughts on the article. If you forget to put quotation marks around a quote, you might be tempted a few days later to assume that was your paraphrase. You can end up failing a paper and getting in academic trouble for mistakes like that.

- Cite as you go. When you're writing the paper, you might think you're too in-the-zone to cite, but you have to. At least put the author's name and page number there. You can come back and double check that citations are in the right format (MLA, Chicago, APA...) during the editing process, but trying to cite after you write means that you'll miss something. Moreover, if you're on a tight deadline, it often means you turn in a paper with the kind of errors like those explained in the bullet point above that can get you in trouble.

Note-Taking Strategies

- A double-entry notebook

When Karma was doing her master's degree, she filled several double entry notebooks (her master's project was a whole book long). On one side of the page, she would write the quote, summary, or paraphrase, noting which she was doing, and on the other, she would write notes to herself about the authors' points. Sometimes, she wrote a note about how she wanted to use that quote in the beginning of Chapter Three. Sometimes, she wrote about how the author missed a point. Sometimes, she wrote about how the authors she was writing about agreed and disagreed with each other and where she fit in to the debate they were having.

- A graphic organizer

You can also take notes in tabular form using a simple graphic organizer. Table 5.1 shows three entries of a graphic organizer Melissa used when conducting research for a paper on the memorialization of Japanese American internment during World War II. Note that, like the double-entry notebook, the graphic organizer helped

Source/Citation	Summary
Chung Simpson, Carolyn. *An Absent Presence: Japanese Americans in Postwar American Culture, 1945–1960.* Duke University Press, 2001.	Intro and CH 1: The author applies Marita Sturken's concept of "absent presence" to the manner in which internment is dealt with in academic and public history. Overall, she shows that, despite the many books written about the internment, within broader histories of the war or postwar era, it is often not mentioned or only lightly referenced. Chung argues, nonetheless, that internment "haunts" a number of issues/events of the postwar era—it's an unspoken memory in a number of cultural productions.
Gessner, Ingrid. *From Sites of Memory to Cybersights: (Re)Framing Japanese American Experiences.* American Studies: A Monograph Series, 2007.	CH 1 Detailed history of the internment and the establishment of internment memorials. CH 2 Covers the history of Manzanar Relocation Center becoming a National Park Service memorial site and also the history of the controversy of the memorial in Washington, DC.
Reeves, Richard. *Infamy: The Shocking Story of the Japanese American Internment in World War II.* Holt & Company, 2015.	General history written for a general audience. Includes photos, map of camp locations throughout the US, and map of Manzanar. CH 1 covers some basic factual details: Under Executive Order 9066 (19 Feb. 1942) (about 10 weeks after Pearl Harbor, 7 Dec. 1941) more than 120,000 Nikkei were incarcerated in 10 relocation centers and several prisons throughout the US. None was charged with a crime of espionage or sabotage. CH 2 covers the period between Pearl Harbor and EO 9066, including some discussion of how the Japanese Americans had been treated prior to the war.

Quotes	Notes
P. 3: "The internment exists everywhere in the immediate postwar as a vacated history, which Sturken likens to the 'traces of events for which there have been no camera images' or narratives." P. 4: "This study approaches the analysis of Japanese Internment as a project in understanding how history and memory are negotiated when the need to remember an event challenges the ideals of democratic nationalism and the narrative unit of nation that historical discourses ostensibly provide."	This book could provide a useful theoretical framework that I could apply to my analysis of the memorial sites. Read also Sturken's article in which she introduces the concept of "absent presence."
P. 13: "Michael Kammen counts Manzanar among the 'parks with an edge' to them." These sites "expose episodes in American past about which a consensus does not exist."	Look for Kammen's book. Useful material in CH 2 about places of memory becoming places of forgetting as well. In CH 1 & 2: Pay attention to the terminology the author uses to describe modalities of public memory.
P. xv: "The dangers of history repeating itself seem greater given that this story is often forgotten or treated as a footnote in the larger mostly heroic description of World War II found in American history books."	Makes an excellent point that now is an important time to revisit this historical event because of the current public/political rhetoric about Muslims and Mexicans. It seems as if, based on info in CH 1, the Nisei, as citizens, were allowed to own property prior to EO 9066 and that they lost it when they were sent to the camps. Need to double check this to make sure I've got it right.

Table 5.1   Sample graphic organizer

Melissa organize and distinguish between her own ideas (in the "Notes" column) and the authors' ideas and words.

• Note-taking software

Most universities subscribe to a note-taking software for their students. Endnote, for example, is commonly made available for all students at universities. Libraries hold workshops on how to use the software. Ask your librarian which software your university might have for free (well, it's part of what you get with your tuition) for you to use.

Endnote and similar software allow you to make notes on particular works. You can often import items from your library search directly into the software, meaning that if you found seven articles for your essay, you can have Endnote create entries with the information you can see in the library search: the bibliographic data, the abstract, sometimes the whole pdf. There will also be a space to write notes as you read the piece.

The advantages are that you create a searchable database for yourself. Who was the author who said so and so was "absurd"? If you've quoted that word, you can search for it. You can also link Word to the note-taking software and export citations in whatever format your professor requires (as long as Endnote has that format as an option).

Remember to input the genre correctly. Endnote needs to know whether this is an article in a journal or in a newspaper to export the citation correctly. You will also usually need to do a final format check at the end of editing the paper. Note-taking software and computer programs that create bibliographies for you usually mess up in two ways: they spit out the citation single-spaced (and in many citation formats, they need to be double-spaced) and without special indentation (while many formats require hanging/reverse indentation).

CHAPTER SIX

Other Sources
Interviews, Focus Groups, and Surveys

A. Introduction

Thus far, we have been discussing sources that are published in one form or another: books, articles in academic journals, newspapers, magazines, encyclopedia entries, and websites. However, in our everyday lives, we regularly rely on information that comes from unpublished sources as well.

Healthcare providers are sources of information for patients. Financial advisors provide information for people who are planning for retirement. A woman who is pregnant for the first time might seek information from friends and family members who have already experienced pregnancy and childbirth. A dog owner might talk to other pet owners in his neighborhood about the best place to board his Labrador during an upcoming vacation. As a university student, you may rely upon information from academic advisers about which courses to take or information from other students about which campus organizations to join. In addition, when you're starting to think about your post-graduate career, you might seek the insights of people who are already established in your prospective field about what it takes to land that first job.

These everyday exchanges are a form of research; the people seeking information are conducting research, and those who provide the information, based on their own expertise or experiences, are sources.

Professional writers also recognize that ordinary people, who may not have published a word (in the conventional sense of publishing), can be rich sources of information. For this reason, they often seek opportunities to collect unpublished ideas, insights, and opinions, but in a more formal manner, through interviews, focus groups, and surveys. In this chapter, we introduce you to these forms of research and provide you with some tips about how to conduct such research yourself.

B. The Value of Interviews and Focus Groups as Sources

You may have previously thought of interviewing as the domain of journalists or as part of the process a job seeker has to do to get a position, but interviewing is also a common research method used by experts in many academic disciplines and professional fields.

Researchers in fields such as sociology, education, and public health frequently interview subjects as a method of collecting primary source information. Technical writers often interview technical or scientific experts to communicate effectively the experts' inventions or research to a non-expert audience. Healthcare professionals will interview a patient and sometimes members of the patient's family if they want to write a case study on the patient's health problem, treatment, and prognosis.[1]

Academic and professional writers might interview people for many reasons. There may be no existing primary or secondary sources on the research topic. The researcher may know of individuals who made important discoveries or have had unique experiences that have value for readers. Or a researcher may be investigating a new social phenomenon or public initiative and want to learn how individuals are responding to or participating in it. Such was the case for Eric Klinenberg when he was conducting research for his book, *Going Solo: The Extraordinary Rise and Surprising Appeal of Living Alone*. He and his research team conducted 300 interviews with people living on their own. Information he collected through these interviews led him to his thesis: people "going solo" today aren't nearly as socially isolated as many had previously assumed.

Interviewing provides researchers with information they can't get elsewhere. Interviews give insight into under-studied topics, offer researchers the opportunity to examine the motivations and points of view of the people they interview, and sometimes uncover the unexpected. Klinenberg went into his research assuming that people living alone were more socially isolated than those who lived with others, but his interviews led to the opposite conclusion. Similarly, a

---

1 Case studies are frequently published in peer-reviewed medical journals, but they have become a popular genre among non-expert readers as well. Atul Gawande, the surgeon and author we mentioned in Chapter One, has published a number of case studies in *The New Yorker*, and his collection of case studies, *Complications*, was a bestseller.

British research team conducting interviews with school children regarding their food choices and preferences discovered a factor that they hadn't given much weight to prior to the interviews: the role that peer pressure plays in the food choices children make (Stewart et al.). They only realized how significant this influence was by interviewing the children.

Interviewing is considered a form of *qualitative research* because it is exploratory and intended to capture the feelings, beliefs, opinions, and singular experiences of individuals, as opposed to *quantitative research*, which gathers numeric data and often involves statistical analysis.

Focus groups are another form of qualitative research, which gather a group of people to get a collective sense of their opinions on a topic. Members of the research team serve as moderators of the focus group. They introduce the topic and facilitate the discussion. Focus groups are typically taped so that the research team can later analyze the discussion.

Focus groups were first pioneered by market researchers, and they are still commonly used in this profession. Melissa once participated in a market research focus group. The topic? Ice cream! An ice cream brand was considering adding a new flavor to its existing offerings. They wanted to know how consumers felt about the flavor and how it held up to flavors offered by competing brands. For two hours, Melissa and her lucky focus group peers got to sample different ice creams and discuss their preferences. During the discussion, the moderators said little, did not reveal their preferences, and did not reveal the brand names or which flavor was the one being tested. These strategies were employed by the moderators to avoid influencing the discussion, even though their goal was to gather the participants' subjective opinions and preferences.

Academic researchers, government entities, and other organizations with an interest in public opinion soon caught on to the value of the focus group and began using the method to assess attitudes toward issues more serious than ice cream, such as dental hygiene, public transportation, and homelessness. The study abroad program at our university uses focus groups to assess students' attitudes toward proposals for new study abroad courses.

If academic researchers have used interviews or focus groups while conducting their research, they will signal this in the abstract and provide information about how the subjects were chosen and how the interviews or focus groups were conducted. Sometimes they will also include a list of questions as a supplementary document.

C. Effective and Ethical Procedures for Conducting Interviews

When journalists interview people for news articles, they are usually under deadline pressure. Current events articles must be published within a day of the event; otherwise, the news is no longer current. While ethical journalists make every effort quote interviewees accurately, mistakes do sometimes happen due to the turnaround time. When this occurs—for example, a city official complains to the newspaper that she's been misquoted—a reputable newspaper will print a retraction or correction of the quotation in the next issue.

Reputable online news sources will make the correction in the article itself, but will also include a note at the bottom of the webpage indicating the correction. Here's a funny one that appears at the end of David Rosenberg's *Slate* article on pole dancing:

> Correction, April 3, 2014: This post originally quoted photographer Tom Sanders as saying it takes him five years to get on the dance floor. It takes him five beers.

Years or beers? You can see how Rosenberg might honestly have misheard Sanders's statement.

The presence of retractions or corrections is a sign of the reliability of the news source: the editors are complying with their ethical obligation to correct mistakes. A less reliable news source might not make the effort, and a disreputable source might even be purposefully manipulating the story they're reporting.

When academic researchers conduct interviews, they are under less time pressure than news reporters are, and they generally adhere to the following guidelines for undertaking ethical and effective interviews. If you're evaluating a research article that relies upon information derived from interviews to support its findings, you should check the methodology section to see how well the researchers followed these guidelines. You should follow them as well if you plan to do interviews for your research.

Planning for the Interview

- Conduct advance research on the topic of the interview.

Academic writers often signal their knowledge on the topic in a mini-literature review at the beginning of their articles. You also need to be informed before you begin your interviews.

When we ask the students in our writing in the health professions courses to interview a patient for a case study, we encourage them to first do some research on the patient's health concern. This enables the students to formulate effective interview questions and respond appropriately during the interview.

- Select the demographic for the interviewees.

If you are conducting multiple interviews on the same topic, choose interviewees from a comparable demographic. Comparative results of interviews are only reliable if the people interviewed share some common characteristics or backgrounds. For instance, the researchers studying children's food preferences interviewed only children ages 6–11 living in a particular region of Wales.

- Create a list of open-ended questions.

Effective interview questions will be open-ended, meaning that they will elicit fuller, more developed answers, as opposed to "yes" or "no" responses.

> Closed-ended question: Do you like the healthy foods that your parents encourage you to eat?
>
> Open-ended question: How do you feel about the healthy foods that your parents encourage you to eat?

- Eliminate or revise leading questions.

A leading question is one that encourages an interviewee to respond in a way that yields answers confirming the interviewer's hypothesis. If the results of interviews are to be trusted, the questions must be stated objectively. Remember that Klinenberg's interviews led him to answers he hadn't expected. If his questions had been too leading, he might never have discovered the phenomenon that became central to his book.

> Leading question: How do you deal with loneliness while living alone?
>
> Non-leading question: How would you describe your feelings about living alone?

- Organize the questions in a logical order.

Think about the flow of a conversation. Starting with more general questions and then leading into more specific ones is usually effective. Grouping questions by themes is also a good choice.

Pro-Tip!

End your interview with a *very* open-ended question. Every experienced interviewer we know has had the experience of learning something entirely unexpected but crucial from interviewees. In anticipation of this, you should plan to conclude your interview with a question like "What is something important that I haven't thought to ask you about?" or "What should my readers know that we haven't already covered?"

- Prepare a written statement about the purpose of the interview and the research it will inform.[2]
- Prepare a consent form. Consent forms typically ask interviewees to acknowledge a number of things, including the following:
  - They have voluntarily agreed to be interviewed.
  - They may decline to answer some questions.
  - They can withdraw from the interview at any point.
  - They agree to have the interview recorded.
  - They understand how information from their interview will be used in the research.
  - They give permission for the interviewer to quote them in any subsequent publication.

If the interviews involve children under the age of consent (18 in the US, 18 or 19 in Canada, depending on the province), the forms must be signed by the children's parents. The researchers conducting the study of children's food preferences followed this protocol.

---

2 To see a sample purpose statement and consent form please go to the *Who's Your Source?* website.

During the Interview

- Arrive on time for the interview, and don't forget to bring your prepared documents (questions, consent form, statement of purpose).
  - Remember that the interviewee is volunteering his time to help you with your research. His time is just as valuable as yours.
- Present the interviewee with your written statement about the purpose of the interview. Give her time to read it and ask questions.
- Ask the interviewee to read and sign the consent form.
- Record the interview, but also take notes. Sometimes recordings fail due to technological problems or user error.
  - One of Melissa's students learned this lesson the hard way; he relied only on recording his interview on his smartphone. The next day he jumped into a swimming pool with his smartphone in his pocket. Whoops!
- Adopt an open, but neutral demeanor during the interview.
- Make eye contact. Encourage the interviewee to continue speaking by using verbal affirmations ("I see," "mmm hmm") but avoid influencing their responses by smiling, frowning, or expressing too much enthusiasm for a particular answer.
- Be an attentive, active listener.

Although you should ask the interviewee your prepared questions, you should also be open to asking follow-up questions or rephrasing questions if it seems that the interviewee doesn't understand.

Pay attention to the interviewee's body language as well as his words. Facial expressions, eye contact, and posture can provide insight into how the interviewee is feeling. If at any point, the interviewee seems to be in distress, offer to conclude early.

- Thank the interviewee for her time and ask for permission to contact her again should you have any follow up questions.

After the Interview

- Review the interview notes as soon as possible after the interview, adding details that you may not have captured at the time.
- Protect the interviewee's privacy.
  - ○ Make sure that your notes are stored in a secured place. Do not use the interviewee's real name when writing a report or article unless you have obtained signed permission to do so.

D. The Value of Surveys as Sources

You've probably answered a survey or two. Maybe a survey popped up in the social media platform you use: it was on a topic that interested you, so you responded. Perhaps you've also answered political polls during election seasons. Your family likely participates in the Census Bureau surveys that are distributed to households at regular intervals in Canada and the US.

Surveys are a form of *quantitative research*, so named because they collect numerical data. Market researchers use surveys to figure out how to create and promote products that will appeal to a large number of consumers. The UK-based YouGov market research team collects survey data on everything from Britain's favorite pizza topping to how many Brits have at least one smart home device. Census surveys collect data on respondents' age, race, marital status, income, employment, languages spoken, education level, and family size, which governments use to get a sense of the population at large and to create programs that will benefit citizens and residents.

Professional and academic writers also use statistics gleaned from surveys. In *Going Solo*, Eric Klinenberg cites statistics from a variety of surveying organizations, including the US Census Bureau, the Pew Research Center, Euromonitor International, Statistics Canada, and the World Health Organization. Data from these organizations enabled Klinenberg to establish the upward trend toward living alone and to support his argument that those living alone are neither lonelier nor less healthy than their cohabiting counterparts are. As you may recall from Chapter One, Melissa used survey data from Statista when she conducted her Reality Check: no, it's not likely that she's eaten 10,000 bananas in her lifetime!

Around tax time in 2017, NPR broadcast (and later published on their website) an article about tax literacy in the US. The writer, Danielle Kurtzleben, relied on data from the public opinion research organization Ipsos, which had conducted a survey at the request of NPR, about what Americans know about US tax policy. The overall answer: not much. We found the responses to two of the survey questions particularly noteworthy:

> Sixty-five per cent of respondents agreed with the statement "the estate tax should be abolished."

> Seventy-six per cent of respondents agreed with the statement "the death tax should be abolished."

Can you spot the problem here? The estate tax and the death tax are two ways of naming the same policy. Did Ipsos make a mistake when creating the survey questions? Not at all. These questions were designed to find out if respondents understood that the estate tax and the death tax are the same thing. Apparently, many did not.

Without this source of information, Kurtzleben might have relied upon anecdotal evidence or interviews with experts about Americans' lack of tax policy knowledge, but the survey data, collected from more than 1,000 respondents, made the point quite persuasively.

Additionally, the survey results provided evidence for a point that savvy evaluators of political discourse have long suspected: the language that politicians use to describe policy has a great impact on how the public reacts to it.

Politicians in favor of repealing the estate tax began referring to it as the death tax in the 1990s.[3] "Death tax" is an example of a dysphemism, like a euphemism,[4] that has taken a gloomy turn. "Death," a word with negative connotations, is being substituted for the official policy term, "estate." After decades of usage, it's no surprise that people are confused about the death tax, nor that they are more likely to favor repealing it than the estate tax, a notion that Kurtzleben comments on in her article.

Reality Check

Politicians also use polling and survey data to learn about the concerns of their constituents and to see how they're stacking up compared to other candidates. You should be prepared, however, to conduct a Reality Check any time politicians cite survey statistics that show support for their own agendas, particularly if their supporters have had a hand in creating the survey questions. Unlike academic researchers or independent research organizations, politicians do not always follow the rule about avoiding leading questions. They may, rather, purposefully phrase questions to yield favorable answers. They are likewise often guilty of taking survey data out of context. One can imagine, for instance, an anti-estate-tax politician citing the 76 per cent of respondents who favor repealing the death tax, without explaining that the overall takeaway from the Ipsos survey was how uninformed Americans are about tax policy.

Vocabulary note

A poll typically only asks one question, whereas a survey will present multiple questions.

---

3 See *Investopedia*, "Death Taxes."
4 Euphemism works in the opposite direction, substituting a less harsh or less offensive word for the original term. For example, sometimes people will say that someone has "passed" to soften the delivery of the news of a death.

If you are writing a paper for which survey statistics would serve as a useful source of information or evidence, you can access reliable survey data collected by government entities and impartial research organizations on the internet, some of which we've already named in this section. These groups make their data available in the interest of transparency and public service.

E. Survey Genres: Naturalistic Observation, Questionnaires, Likert Scales

When there is no existing survey data on a particular research topic, academic researchers may create and distribute their own surveys, analyze the data, and incorporate the results into their writing. The methodology section of the resulting research article will provide details about the type of survey used and the number of respondents.

When the two of us were preparing to write this book, Karma created a questionnaire to learn what writing students on the University of California, Davis campus did and didn't know about using sources in their own writing. Analyzing the collected data helped us figure out which topics we needed to address. Some of our students have also created their own surveys when engaged in research for our courses. For example, when Melissa's student Kim-Thu Pham was writing a paper about campus bias against beach cruiser-style bicycles, she had a sense that some of this bias was gendered: she'd observed that more female than male students rode beach cruisers on campus. However, one person's off-hand observation is not enough to persuade readers. She needed evidence, so she created a "pencil-and-paper survey of traffic" at the busiest bike circle on the UC Davis campus, the results of which showed that "74% of cruiser riders are female" (Pham 62).

If you've reached a dead end when searching the library sources for information on your topic, you might want to try collecting data yourself using one of the three following surveying methods.

Naturalistic Observation Survey

Kim-Thu's survey is an example of the naturalistic observational surveying method. For such surveys, researchers position themselves in a public place to observe the behaviors of passersby who are unaware they are being observed. For example, Miguel A. Figliozzi and Chawalit Tipagornwong, two civil engineering researchers, conducted a naturalistic observational survey to assess vehicle violations at a pedestrian crosswalk at a busy intersection in Portland, Oregon. The researchers discovered that drivers of large vehicles, such as SUVs, are less likely than drivers of other types of vehicles to yield at pedestrian crosswalks.

Figliozzi and Tipagornwong had more resources available to them than Kim-Thu; they were able to videotape an intersection over an extended period and later count the number of cars, vehicle types, and violations. Kim-Thu had only paper and pencil to record the data. Nonetheless, her survey results, along with several other aspects of her research-supported paper, were enough to persuade not only Kim-Thu's classmates and instructor, but also the judges of the *Prized Writing* competition on our campus. Her article was published in the 2013–14 volume of *Prized Writing*. You can read her complete article in Chapter Eight.

The naturalistic observation survey is a good choice if you have only a small number of behavioral data points to record in a small number of categories (e.g., type of bicycle and gender of rider). If you choose this method, you'll need to position yourself at a time and place that will show you a representative slice of the population. There's no sense situating yourself outside of the campus library at 9:00 a.m. on a Sunday morning if you're trying to assess library foot traffic, unless you're trying to show how few people use the library at that time!

If you want to gather more nuanced information than a naturalistic observation survey would collect, you might try a questionnaire or a Likert scale survey.

Questionnaires

Questionnaires may include multiple choice or "open response" questions or both. An open response question allows survey respondents to write a sentence or more in response to the question, whereas multiple-choice questions offer three to five pre-written answers.

A questionnaire could provide you with insight into not only how many students are using the library at 9:00 a.m. on Sunday mornings, but also why. See below.

1. Do you ever visit the campus library at 9:00 a.m. on Sunday mornings?
   □ Yes
   □ No
If yes, please answer questions 2 and 3. If no, please answer question 4.

2. How frequently do you visit the library on Sundays at 9:00 a.m.?
   □ Once a month.
   □ Twice a month.
   □ Three times a month.
   □ Every Sunday.

3. Which statement best describes your reason for using the library at 9:00 a.m. on Sundays:
   □ I like to get a head start on studying for the week.
   □ The library is quiet at that time.
   □ I don't have to wait in line to get on the library computers at that time.
   □ I do my best thinking at that time.
   □ Other.

4. Which statement best describes your reason for *not* using the library at 9:00 a.m. on Sundays:
   □ I prefer to sleep in on Sunday mornings.

☐ I prefer to spend the weekend with my family or friends.
☐ I reserve Sundays for rest and relaxation.
☐ I didn't know the library was open at that time.
☐ I never go to the library.
☐ Other.

In a survey like this, the "other" options in questions three and four might be followed with an open response prompt in which respondents can add their own reason (e.g., "If you chose 'other,' please explain"). Note, however, that individual responses can be quite disparate and idiosyncratic (e.g., "Because my ex-boyfriend is usually at the library at that time, and I'm trying to avoid him"). You might gather unexpected responses from these questions, but they will be more challenging to quantify when it's time to analyze your data.

Likert Scales

You've seen Likert[5] scales, even you if didn't previously know what they are called. They're used effectively to assess respondents' preferences, attitudes, or likelihood of doing something. They elicit more nuanced data than would a simple yes or no question. Likert scale surveys present respondents with a question or statement and then offer five to seven different, but simple responses to choose from, as in the example below.

Please check the option that best expresses your response to the following statement: I am likely to visit the campus library on Sunday mornings.				
☐	☐	☐	☐	☐
Strongly Agree	Agree	Unsure	Disagree	Strongly Disagree
1	2	3	4	5

Table 6.1

---

5 Likert is always capitalized because the scale is named after the psychologist who invented it, Rensis Likert.

Because each response on the Likert scale is assigned a numerical value (here 1–5), Likert scale data are easy to quantify.

F. Effective and Ethical Procedures for Conducting Surveys

If you're interested in conducting your own survey as a part of your research, there are a number of guidelines to follow for doing so effectively and ethically.

- Choose the appropriate survey method for the type of data you want to collect.
- For an observational survey, choose the categories of behavior you'll be observing and create a simple table (on paper or a laptop) for recording numbers.
- For questionnaires or Likert scale surveys, compose effective and ethical questions.
  - Effective survey questions are designed to elicit the information that you need for your research. They should be direct and unambiguous. If you must use a term that may be unfamiliar to some respondents, define it within the question.
  - Ethical survey questions, as in an interview, are not leading.
- Ask questions about respondents' identities (e.g., age, race, gender) only if these demographics are relevant to your research.
- Present your questions in a logical order, so that one question leads fluidly to the next.
- Pre-test your survey. Researchers using surveys often pre-test their surveys with a small group and then revise any confusing, unproductive, or leading questions before conducting the survey proper. You can take a similar approach by getting feedback on your questions from a small group of friends or classmates.
- For ethical reasons, you can't revise or add questions after you've started to collect responses: your data across responses won't be comparable.

- At the beginning of the survey, present brief instructions (e.g., "Please check the option that best expresses your opinion on the following points").
- Also at the beginning of the survey, provide the respondent with an estimate for how long the survey will take. People are more likely to respond to a survey if it will only take five to seven minutes. If your survey will take longer than that, be upfront about it. People will be less likely to quit a longer survey before completing it if they know ahead of time how long it is.
- Ask for permission to quote. If you are using any open response prompts (e.g., "Please explain your answer to question 2"), and you would like to quote some responses, you must ask for permission within the survey itself. For example, at the end of the student survey that we mentioned earlier, Karma included the question, "May I quote you (anonymously) in my research?" If a survey respondent answers no to this question, there are absolutely no circumstances in which it would be ethically acceptable to quote him.
- Plan for a low response rate. Recent social science research has shown that survey response rate is typically low, with rates ranging from 12 per cent to 55 per cent. To get the number of responses you'd like, you'll need to get the survey out to many more potential respondents.

A final note about conducting ethical interviews and surveys. When university researchers plan to use human subjects in their studies, including when they are using interviews and surveys as their research methods, they must first submit their research proposals to an ethics review committee. These committees are known as institutional review boards (IRB) in the US and research ethics boards (REB) in Canada. The purpose of the review is to ensure that the researchers are abiding by ethical standards and will do no harm to the study participants. Undergraduate students are not typically required to get IRB/

REB approval for research they're conducting for courses. If you're unsure about the requirements at your university, check with your instructor.

G. How to Use Interviews and Surveys Effectively in Your Writing

After you've completed your interviews or survey and analyzed the responses, consider the following as you incorporate this source material into your writing.

Interviews

• Quote sparingly.

The biggest mistake our students make when incorporating interview information is over-quoting. Your paper should not look like a transcript of your entire interview. Take a hint from professional writers—quote your interviewees only when they have:

- Stated something so eloquently that you wouldn't do justice to it in a paraphrase.
- Said something that serves to characterize them in a distinct and compelling manner.
- Presented an idea or opinion that runs contrary to expectations.
- Expressed an opinion that supports your argument or helps you to develop it.

Even in these instances, you should aim to quote only a sentence or two at a time. Use paraphrase to fill in the rest of the details and be sure to also present your readers with enough context for the quotation that they can understand it. Say, for instance, you've interviewed a geneticist and you want to quote her opinion: "In the near future, CRISPR genome editing will allow us to cure many mental illnesses." You'll need to explain to your readers what CRISPR genome editing is. And we wish you luck with that!

Do not quote interviewees on uncontroversial facts, especially facts that are easily found in other sources.

If you'd like to hear how a professional writer uses material from interviews in his writing, check the *Who's Your Source?* website for a link to Michael Pollan's talk with undergraduate writing students at our university.

- Don't forget about ethos.

If you've interviewed an expert, let your readers know. It can be done simply as you're introducing a quotation: According to Dr. Ana Garcia, genetics professor at McGill University, "In the near future, CRISPR genome editing will allow us to cure many mental illnesses."

- Don't put words in your interviewees' mouths.

Everything that you put between quotation marks must be the exact words an interviewee said. It's acceptable to change or leave out a few words in a quotation to integrate it more effectively into your own sentence, but only if you use the appropriate punctuation (brackets or ellipses) to indicate to the reader that you've changed the original wording. We'll cover the mechanics of this move in Chapter Nine.

If your notes are sketchy or you don't have a clear recording of what an interviewee said, you will need to paraphrase instead.

- Don't reveal your interviewees' identities if they haven't given you permission.

If your interviewee has not signed consent for you to use his name in your writing, don't do it. Instead, give the interviewee a pseud-onym and let your reader know. The first time you use the pseud-onym, insert a footnote stating, "The name of the interviewee has been changed to protect his privacy."

Surveys

• Use charts and tables to convey numerical data.

If you have a lot of numerical data (i.e., more than two or three data points) to convey, presenting it in a visual format will make it easier for your readers to absorb. See Chapter Seven for guidelines on using visuals.

• Don't assume the numbers stand for themselves.

Treat numerical data, including data represented in visuals, as if it were a quotation. Just as a quotation alone does nothing for your argument until you explain how it advances your point, numbers alone won't make your paper more persuasive. Introduce your sur-vey data with an explanation of what they represent, and follow up with an explanation of what you want your readers to take from the numbers.

• Quote sparingly.

If you asked open-ended questions, and have permission to quote respondents, pick a few quotations that are rich in content and representative of the data trends. You might also include a quota-tion that illustrates an outlier position.

• Be honest upfront about the sample size.

Have you ever read an advertisement that said something like this: "Nine out of ten dentists surveyed recommend Brand X dental floss"? Did you then ask yourself, "How many dentists were surveyed?" We hope so. Brand X hopes consumers will understand this statement to mean that 90 per cent of dentists recommend Brand X, but that's not necessarily the case. They may have only surveyed 10 dentists, which is not a good sample size.

If you're using data conducted by a surveying organization, check to see how many people participated in the survey and pass this information on to your readers. For example, you might say, "According to the Canadian Bureau of International Education, 60 per cent of the more than 14,000 international students they surveyed 'indicated an intention to seek permanent residence in Canada.'" If the survey does not indicate the number of respondents, the source may not be reliable.

The same goes for you if you conducted your own survey. Be upfront with your readers. Tell them how many people you surveyed or risk being viewed as unreliable. You should also tell readers how you conducted your survey, either in the body of your paper, a footnote, or the appendix.

Visual Rhetoric

A. Introduction

In *Ways of Seeing*, art historian John Berger writes, "Seeing comes before words" (7). By this, he means that, as infants, we humans learn to negotiate our worlds via visual cues long before we understand language and, further, that sight remains our primary sense of understanding and interpreting what is around us. With this in mind, check out Figure 7.1 below. Can you tell what this document is, even though it isn't written in English?

Lorem Ipsum

Dolor Sit Amet

Consectetur Adipiscing Elit   x

Nunc Sed Luctus Dui   f

Etiam Pharetra Ligula
*Pellentesque habitant morbi tristique senectus et netus et
malesuada fames ac turpis egestas*   ib

Faucibus Dictum
Aenean lobortis facilisis odio, et ornare elit facilisis   ib

Tellus Sem Pulvinar
Curabitur vel massa id justo vulputate ullamcorper at in nunc   f

Massa Diam Sed

Nullam vestibulum pulvinar, si dunisi   if

Donec in nisl accumsan sodales   al

Maecenas tempor lorem odio   al

Donec pellentesque consequat volutpat
Duis vestibulum aliquam velit a volutpat, nunc nisi neque   db

Vehicula at egestas ac, dignissim vel ex
In ut orci placerat, imperdiet ante at, volutpat tellus   db

Tempor Quam

Aliquam est odio   m

Laoreet at massa   m

Donec posuere lacus   j

At euismod lacus diam quis odio. Maecenas at egestas purus.

Figure 7.1   Can you guess what this is?

If you guessed that Figure 7.1 is a restaurant menu, you'd be on the right track. What led you to this conclusion? You've likely seen a number of restaurant menus in your life, and you recognize the genre conventions in this example. The title of the restaurant is centered at the top. The underlined words indicate course categories (appetizers, main courses, desserts) and the figures on the right seem to indicate prices.

You might have also guessed that this is a menu for a fine-dining restaurant as opposed to a casual-dining establishment like a diner or a pub. What are the signs? The title of the restaurant is presented in a fancy script font and the number of selections available for each course is few. A diner menu would likely be printed in a more casual font and offer many more choices.

In fact, this isn't (yet) a real menu. It's written in Lorem Ipsum,[1] a dummy language based on Latin, which graphic designers and others in the desktop publishing industry use when designing documents. They insert Lorem Ipsum into a document when the real text is not yet available so that they can see what the document will look like when it is complete.

We put you through this brief exercise to introduce you to the concept of visual rhetoric, the idea that visuals of all sorts can have a persuasive impact on the audience. Lorem Ipsum doesn't mean anything, but you were persuaded by the document design to believe that this is a menu.

Everything from document and website design to photos and charts can persuade readers to interpret sources in particular ways. Recall from Chapter Three, Karma's student's comment on the visual appearance of *The Onion*: "If you don't read any of the words, this looks totally true." See for yourself in the header of this satire website.

---

1 If you've ever used a PowerPoint template to create a presentation, you've encountered Lorem Ipsum. PowerPoint uses Lorem Ipsum to show you what your slides will look like if you use the fonts they've preset for each template.

Figure 7.2   *The Onion* website header

The Onion's header doesn't look very different from the headers of real news sites. Moving on to the words, the menu bar lists a number of categories that you would find on news sites: politics, sports, entertainment, etc.

These visual aspects of *The Onion* contribute to some readers' misinterpretation of the site as a real news source, but an attentive reader, with a good sense of humor and some understanding of internet lingo, would be able to tell the difference by the time she gets to "clickhole." You're not going to see that in the menu bar of *The Wall Street Journal* or *The Toronto Globe and Mail*. The clever editors of *The Onion* are signifying that their site is for fun by playing upon the phrases "click bait" and "down the rabbit hole," which is where we all go when we click too many times on the attention-grabbing headlines that pop up in our web browsers.

You've probably heard the phrase "a picture is worth a thousand words." Clichéd though it may be, this phrase holds some truth. For many readers, visual rhetoric is even more persuasive than verbal rhetoric. Thus, you must evaluate the visual aspects of your sources and know how to use visual rhetoric ethically and effectively in your writing. In the next few sections, we give you some tips on the most common genres of visuals you will encounter.

B. Charts, Tables, and Graphs

Writers employ charts, graphs, and tables to convey quantitative data to audiences in an accessible and easy to absorb manner. Consider the following two options, a data narrative and a data table (see Table 7.1), for conveying survey results from the Canadian Bureau of International Education (CBIE).

Data Narrative: When international students were asked about their post-graduation plans, 49 per cent said that they planned to work in Canada and become permanent residents. Another 21 per cent said that they intended to work in Canada for up to three years before returning home. Those who reported that they planned to look for work in their home countries or another country make up another 9 per cent and 5 per cent, respectively. Only 3 per cent said that they would return to a previous job in their home country, and 13 per cent responded that they do not have any work-related plans.

Employment plans following current program of study	
Work permanently in Canada (become a permanent resident of Canada)	49%
Work for up to three years in Canada, before returning home	21%
None, I do not have any work-related plans	13%
Look for work in my home country	9%
Look for work in another country that is neither Canada nor my home country	5%
Return to previous job in my home country	3%

Table 7.1   Data table
Source: Canadian Bureau of International Education

Which did you find easier to parse—the data narrative or the data table? Most readers find this kind of data more accessible in tabular form, which is probably why the CBIE chose to present it this way in their report.

If, on the other hand, a writer has only a few numbers to convey to the audience, there's no need to create a visual. For instance, Kim-Thu Pham, whose paper we described in Chapter Six, could have put the data from her survey into a pie chart or a table, but what would be the point? She was able to present the numbers succinctly in two sentences: "A casual pencil-and-paper survey of traffic around the Silo bike circle shows that 74% of cruiser riders are female. This survey was done on a weekday afternoon in the span of half an hour; over one hundred bicycles were counted" (Pham 62).

Tables, charts, and graphs are different genres of data representation. As is the case with texts, writers need to consider the genre conventions if they hope to convey their data effectively in visual form; different kinds of data are best suited to different visual genres. Choose unwisely and you may just confuse your audience.

Pie Charts

The pie chart in Figure 7.3 appeared on the site of the market research company *YouGov*. It was soon re-posted and ridiculed on a several social networking platforms and graphic design sites. Can you tell why?

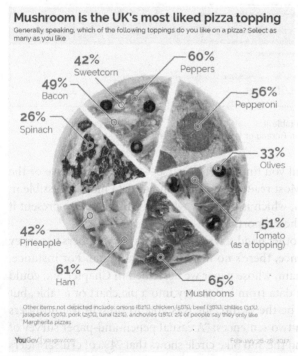

Mushroom is the UK's most liked pizza topping
Generally speaking, which of the following toppings do you like on a pizza? Select as many as you like

42% Sweetcorn
60% Peppers
49% Bacon
56% Pepperoni
26% Spinach
33% Olives
42% Pineapple
51% Tomato (as a topping)
61% Ham
65% Mushrooms

Other items not depicted include: onions (62%), chicken (56%), beef (36%), chillies (31%), jalapeños (30%), pork (25%), tuna (22%), anchovies (18%). 2% of people say they only like Margherita pizzas

YouGov | yougov.com   February 26-28 2017

Figure 7.3   Mushroom is the UK's most liked pizza topping
Source: YouGov.co.uk.com

If your first reaction was "corn on pizza?" we're with you, but that's not what's wrong here. This chart violates several genre conventions of the pie chart:

- The slices of a pie chart must add up to 100 per cent. This one adds up to 485 per cent.
- Each slice must be proportionate to the percentage it represents. Here the slices are all the same size, regardless of whether they are representing 26 per cent or 65 per cent.
- Each slice must represent a single value. Here several of the slices are assigned more than one value. One slice, representing three values, adds up to 151 per cent all by itself.

So what went wrong? We're not debating *YouGov*'s numbers. They typically poll 1,000 to 4,000 people for their surveys, large enough sample sizes from which to draw statistical conclusions. However, the structure of the question they asked for this survey did not yield answers conducive to representing in pie chart form: "Generally speaking, which of the following toppings do you like on a pizza? Select as many as you like." Respondents could choose from not just the toppings shown on the pie chart, but a number of others as well. If you give respondents the opportunity to select more than one option, the total is always going to add up to more than 100 per cent.

This data would have been more effectively represented in a different kind of chart or table. We assume that the folks at *YouGov* know this, but perhaps the temptation to represent the results in a pizza pie chart was just too great given the topic of the survey.

Tables

Tables are the most appropriate choice when you have a large number of data points, when precise numbers are important, such as when you want to present numbers down to the first or second decimal point, or when the difference between the data points is slim.

The table in Table 7.2 presents data from the US Bureau of Labor Statistics on the states with the highest unemployment rates in July 2018.

Highest Unemployment Rates in US by State	
Alaska	6.9%
Arizona	4.6%
Louisiana	4.9%
Mississippi	4.8%
Nevada	4.6%
New Mexico	4.7%
Ohio	4.6%
Washington	4.6%
West Virginia	5.5%

Table 7.2 Organized by state
Source: US Bureau of Labor Statistics

See what happens when the same data is represented in a bar chart (Figure 7.4).

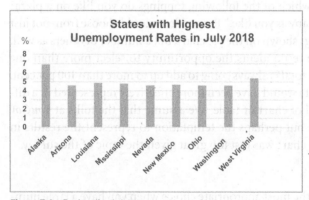

Figure 7.4 Revisualized data
Source: US Bureau of Labor Statistics

Precise values are difficult to discern in bar charts. In this one, there appears to be only a negligible difference between, for example, Louisiana and Mississippi, but we assume that the additional

0.1 per cent unemployment is important to the governor of Louisiana and to an estimated 4,684[2] unemployed people who make up that 0.1 per cent.

Using a table for this type of data is the right choice, but there are still some additional decisions to make regarding how to organize the data. In Table 7.2, we put the data in alphabetical order by state name. In Table 7.3, the data is arranged by rate, highest to lowest.

Highest Unemployment Rates in US by Percentage	
Alaska	6.9%
West Virginia	5.5%
Louisiana	4.9%
Mississippi	4.8%
New Mexico	4.7%
Washington	4.6%
Ohio	4.6%
Nevada	4.6%
Arizona	4.6%

Table 7.3 Organized by percentage
Source: US Bureau of Labor Statistics

How you organize the data in a table depends on who your audience is and how they'll use the data. For instance, Table 7.2 might be more useful than Table 7.3 for a state government employee. He would be able to quickly scan the table to find his state. A federal government employee, however, might prefer the table in Table 7.3 because it would give her a sense of where the greatest unemployment problems exist across the nation. The difference between the two states with the highest unemployment rates is substantial (6.9 per cent and 5.5 per cent), and this is more readily apparent when they are adjacent to one another.

---

2 Number based on current US Census Bureau estimate of Louisiana's population: 4,684,000.

Bar Charts and Line Graphs

Bar charts and line graphs are useful for displaying comparative data, demonstrating how numbers change over time, or pointing out a correlation. They emphasize the shape of the data as opposed to precise numbers. Look at the bar chart in Figure 7.5.

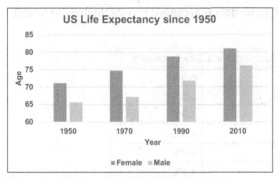

Figure 7.5 US life expectancy 1950–2010
Source: Centers for Disease Control and Prevention

This chart places visual emphasis on the steady upward slope in US life expectancy rates since the 1950s and the enduring gender gap. A line graph (see Figure 7.6) depicting the same numbers has a similar rhetorical impact, though the eye may more easily follow the upward slope as well as the parallel gender progression.

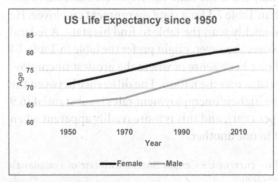

Figure 7.6 US life expectancy, revisualized
Source: Centers for Disease Control and Prevention

While the bar chart and the line graph are effective at illustrating life expectancy changes over time, precise age averages, such as 71.1 for females in 1950, are not discernible in either. If data points like these are important to you or your audience, then a table would be a better choice.

Line graphs are also particularly well suited to show diverging data patterns or trends. For example, see Figure 7.7, for which we created hypothetical data for workers at three different levels of employment: clerical, management, and executive.

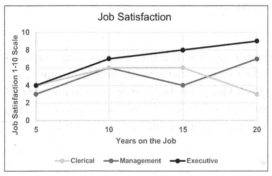

Figure 7.7   Job satisfaction over a 20-year career

C. Ethics and Visual Representations of Data

Numbers often seem to be incontrovertible facts, but they can be manipulated for unethical purposes. Recall the hypothetical example that we offered in Chapter Six: "Nine out of ten dentists surveyed recommend Brand X dental floss." You can't confirm the conclusion that Brand X would like you to make without knowing the total number of dentists surveyed.

Data can also be manipulated in visual representations. See for example, Figure 7.8, which we created using hypothetical data.

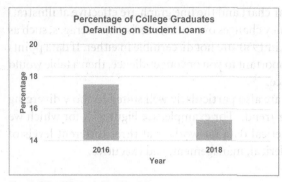

Figure 7.8   Manipulating the data

This bar chart appears to show that the number college graduates who have defaulted on student loans has decreased by more than half from 2016 to 2018. This steep drop, however, is an illusion created by the fact that the y-axis (vertical) does not begin at zero. See what happens in Figure 7.9 when we make the correction:

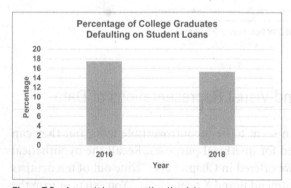

Figure 7.9   Accurately representing the data

This more accurate and ethical representation of the data makes it clearer that the decrease from 2016 to 2018 was less than 3 per cent. Note, however, that it is not always unethical to begin a y-axis at a number higher than zero. For example, the y-axes in Figures 7.5 and 7.6 begin at 60 because the life expectancies between 1950 and 2010 never dropped below 65.

Data distortions can also occur when those who create the visual cherry pick the data that they incorporate into the graph or chart. For example, a few years ago a pie chart (see Figure 7.10) similar to the one that we have recreated below made the rounds on social media accompanied by the question: "Should we outlaw cars?"

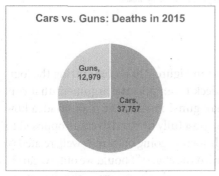

Figure 7.10   Cherry picking the data

Curious about these numbers, we decided to check them against the Centers for Disease Control and Prevention's (CDC) *National Vital Statistics Report*.[3] From this reliable source, we confirmed that there were indeed 37,757 deaths due to vehicular accidents in 2015. However, the number of gun deaths on the chart only included the homicides for the same year. Additional gun deaths included suicides (22,018) and accidental discharge of firearms (489). Adding these numbers significantly changes the pie chart (see Figure 7.11), which we've split apart here to make it easier to see the small slice for accidental deaths:

---

3 See "Table 6: Number of deaths from selected causes, by age: United States, 2015."

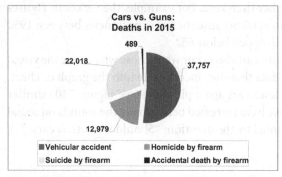

Figure 7.11   Specifying the data

Do you see how the chart in Figure 7.10 is committing the logical fallacy of stacking the deck to support the argument that cars
are three times deadlier than guns? Further, we have no idea how
many people were killed purposefully by car drivers as opposed to
accidents. There's another distortion going on here as well, related to
the question that accompanied the chart: "Should we outlaw cars?"
The implication of this question is that someone is threatening to
outlaw guns, which is not the case in the US, where politicians are
primarily arguing over whether to impose stricter gun-control laws.

D. Guidelines for Evaluating and Creating Effective and Ethical Charts, Tables, and Graphs

When evaluating a table, chart, or graph, use the Three Rs approach.

- Determine the audience, purpose, genre, and context for the
  visual.
- Consider how the visual appeals to ethos, pathos, and logos.
  Visual representations of data tend be effective appeals to logos,
  but if the data have been manipulated in any way, the creator is
  using an appeal to pathos to manipulate *you*.

- If your plausibility alarm bell rings when you examine the visual, as it did for us when we saw the original cars vs. guns pie chart, start looking for reliable data sources that will either confirm or contradict the numbers.

The following questions may assist you in your Three Rs evaluation:

- Does the author reveal the source of the data represented in the table, chart, or graph? Is it a reliable source? Don't trust the data if the source isn't revealed.
- Do you notice any way in which the data could have been manipulated through the design of the visual?
- What argument or narrative is supported by the visual representation data and how?
- Could the argument or narrative be different if the author had chosen a different genre or organized the data in a different way?
- How does the author introduce and discuss the data in the visual? What is she directing you to pay attention to or deflecting you from noticing?

When creating or using tables, charts, or graphs in your own work, do the following:

- Consider how your audience will use the data presented in your visual.
- Choose the genre that is best suited to the data or information that you want to convey and your audience's needs.
- Adhere to the genre conventions for that type of visual.
- Use only data from reliable sources.
- Present the source of your data to the audience.
  - If you are using data collected by another person or an organization, you must cite them, just as you would if you were quoting them. Indicate the source at the bottom of your visual and include an entry for the source on your works cited page.

○ If you are using data that you collected yourself, make that clear in the way that you introduce the visual: "Table 1 presents the results of the survey I conducted..."

- Be honest. Don't fool around with the y-axis or cherry pick your data under the assumption that this will make your point more convincing. This will only damage your credibility as a writer.
- When creating a line graph or bar chart, label your axes so that it's clear what the numbers represent.
- Never give in to the temptation to prioritize cuteness over clarity. Remember that pizza pie chart? The point of creating a table, chart, or graph is to make data more accessible to a reader. Yes, you can make all kinds of fancy 3-D graphs and cute pictograms using software like Microsoft Excel or Google Sheets, but if those options make the data less clear, your visual will not fulfill its purpose.
- If you include more than one visual in your paper, number them ("Table 1, Figure 1," etc.), and reference those numbers in the body of your text, as we did above: "For instance, Table 7.5 might be more useful than Table 7.3 for a state government employee."
- When introducing your visual, provide your audience with a brief explanation of the data, highlighting the most important findings.
- Place your visuals as close as possible to the relevant text. Readers don't want to flip forward to page 8 to look for a chart you mention on page 5.

E. Illustrations, Photos, and Videos

The illustration on the next page, by Gérard DuBois, accompanied the opinion article you read in Chapter One, "How to Stop Overprescribing Antibiotics," by Fox, Linder, and Doctor. Take a few minutes to examine the details.

Did you notice what we noticed? The white coat on the man at the left gives the impression that he is a doctor, which is further

Figure 7.12   Illustration for "How to Stop Overprescribing Antibiotics"
Source: Gérard DuBois, *The New York Times*

supported by the certificates on the wall in the background. The bottle of pills on the desk cues the viewer to understand that the doctor is writing a prescription for a patient on the other side of the desk. The illuminating eye in the desk lamp reinforces Fox, Linder, and Doctor's assertion: when physicians know they're being observed, they are less likely to prescribe unnecessary antibiotics. Is this doctor reconsidering his impulse to prescribe antibiotics? Perhaps: his facial expression seems pensive, uncertain. Overall, DuBois's illustration is an effective visual representation of the authors' argument. On the webpage for this article, the illustration appears at the top. Readers are thus presented with the visual argument prior to the verbal argument.

The photographs and illustrations that accompany many online and print sources serve a variety of rhetorical purposes. They may, like DuBois's illustration, reinforce the argument presented in the text. Some may be used to grab viewers' attention and entice them to read further. For example, Melissa, who can't live without her morning cup of joe, would have likely read the article "The Case for Drinking as Much Coffee as You Like" based on the title alone, but it was the featured photograph of a glossy red mug of steaming coffee that first drew her attention (Abrams). Why was this mug red? Because red has been shown in psychological and market research to be the most visually commanding color on the spectrum. That's why it appears in everything from stop signs to fast food logos.

At other times, photographs and illustrations may be used when words alone are not sufficient to convey critical information. This is the case for the visuals that accompany instructions. See for example the photos accompanying iFixit's instructions for removing the debris extractor from a Roomba.

Figure 7.14 Instructions for removing the debris extractor from a Roomba
Source: iFixit.com

You might not think of instructions as persuasive texts, but they are. Instructions are designed to compel users to do something, fix a household appliance or put together a bookshelf, the right way and with minimal frustration. Notice, for instance, that the photo above is taken from the audience's perspective. The hands in the photo are positioned just as your hands would be if you were following the instructions.

The persuasive impact of photographs and other types of images is most evident in advertising. Corporate advertisers use images of attractive models or celebrities to sell us everything from beer to perfume. Non-profit organizations likewise use images to move us to take action. Think of all of those photos of sad, abandoned animals that you've seen on promotions from places like the Society for the Prevention of Cruelty to Animals. The persuasive intent of such images seems obvious.

However, images can also have a subtler impact on how we interpret the world around us. Often, it takes being shaken out of our typical ways of seeing to notice the extent to which we've been influenced by images around us.

Examine, for instance, the world map below.

Figure 7.14   World map. This map was created in 2007. National borders may have shifted since then due to geopolitical events.
Source: The Spesh Man, WikiMedia Commons

Does this map look strange or *wrong* to you? That's because it's oriented with the South Pole at the top, and most of the world maps we see in our lifetimes are oriented with the North Pole at the top.

While there may be geopolitical reasons why most world maps are oriented toward the north, there are no factual or scientific reasons why this is the case. Nonetheless, seeing the same visual representation time after time has a persuasive impact on us: we unconsciously begin to think of and refer to the north as "up" and south as "down." World maps influence how we think of whole nations and world regions; for instance, Australia is often referred to as the "land down under." That wouldn't be the case if most world maps were oriented with the South Pole at the top.

Moving images (videos) also have a persuasive impact upon us, and they pop up in our online lives daily. A social media video of a cat sitting atop a spinning Roomba makes us laugh. A video of a person walking in a pair of shoes we've looked at online may appear in a sidebar on our computer screens, luring us into considering whether we should buy a pair. Other videos have more complex messages. Take, for example, the four-minute film, "The Majestic Plastic Bag." Watch it for free on *YouTube* at this URL: https://youtube/GLgh9h2ePYw. Do it now. We promise that you'll be entertained.

Did you watch the video? Did you laugh? Let's examine what makes this video effective by considering the rhetorical situation.

While the filmmakers hoped that their viewers would take serious action, they largely worked toward this goal through an appeal to pathos, in the form of humor. Humor loosens up audiences and makes them more receptive to messages. It's hard not to laugh when the narrator's descriptions are strikingly out of proportion ("one of nature's most deadly killers: the teacup Yorkie") or when he offers overly dramatic statements, such as "our highly advanced night-vision cameras have managed to capture for the first time in history a plastic bag in pitch black. Phenomenal." However, the verbal humor works only because it contrasts with the images on the screen: a very cute, playful dog and a blurry blob. As with other visuals, you need to pay attention to the conjunction between words and images to evaluate this film.

Purpose	The purpose of this video is to convince viewers to support a bill to ban plastic bags, but that's not clear until the end when these sentences appear on the screen: "We need your help now to end plastic pollution. Tell your Senator to support [Assembly Bill, or AB] 298 at HealtheBay.org/BagBill. You can make a difference."
Audience	Since AB 298 was a bill in the California state legislature and Heal the Bay is a Los Angeles-based environmental organization, we can surmise that the intended audience is Californians. Although people elsewhere may enjoy *The Majestic Plastic Bag*, Californians are being called to action at the end of the video.

Context	*Physical Context*: This film first debuted at environmental film festivals, but it is now widely available on the internet. If you access it on a site like *YouTube*, promotions for other environmental videos will appear in sidebars, and, immediately after *The Majestic Plastic Bag* ends, another related video will start to play. On our most recent viewing, the next queued video was *Are You Eating Plastic for Dinner?* *Social Context*: This film appeared at a time when concern about the great Pacific garbage patch was increasing and when the state assembly was debating the plastic bag ban.
Genre	*The Majestic Plastic Bag* is an example of a peculiar genre, the nature mockumentary: it mocks the genre of the nature documentary. The film treats the plastic bag as if it were a wild animal and makes use of many of the genre conventions of the nature documentary. The narrator encourages us to personify the bag—"our little bag." We follow the bag on its "migratory" path, watch it fend off "predators" like park rangers and Yorkshire terriers, and view the bag through a "night-vision" camera. The background music swells at (mock) dramatic moments. The filmmakers also likely chose the narrator (actor Jeremy Irons) because his British accent may remind some viewers of David Attenborough, the British naturalist who has narrated countless nature documentaries.

Table 7.4

F. Ethics and Visual Images

As you're evaluating the images you encounter and considering how to use them, remember that an image is still one person's interpretation. This is true even when you're looking at an unaltered photograph. A news photographer must make decisions about what she includes or leaves out of a frame. A newspaper editor must decide which of the photographer's many shots he's going to place next to the front-page story. These choices influence how the audience sees the event represented in the photograph, as does the conjunction between the photo and the words in the article.

Although all images present the perspectives of the person or organization who created them, this does not mean that all images are purposefully manipulative or unethical. No one can escape the fact that he has a perspective.

However, in this age in which photos can easily be altered by anyone with a smartphone or a computer and then spread quickly on the internet, manipulation does occur. For example, the morning after the 2015 terrorist attack in Paris, a photo of the supposed ringleader of the attack appeared on the internet. It depicted a smiling man wearing a suicide vest and holding a Koran in front of him, but the photo was a hoax.

The original photo was a selfie taken by Veerender Jubbal, a Canadian freelance journalist; he's wearing a dastar (the turban worn by Sikhs) and holding not a Koran, but the iPad with which he took the photo in a mirror. Jubbal had tweeted the photo of himself and then someone else had imposed the Koran over the iPad, added the suicide vest, and re-posted it for clearly unethical purposes. Unfortunately, a few legitimate news sources ran the photo without checking its provenance or examining it closely. If the editors had taken the time to evaluate the photo carefully before publishing it, they might have noticed that the presence of both the dastar and the Koran in the image was a sign that it had been manipulated.

The news sources retracted the photo and issued apologies, but the damage had already been done. Jubbal received death threats via Twitter and, some months later, when another terrorist attack happened in Belgium, the manipulated photo re-appeared on social media.[4]

This is, of course, an extreme example. Not all altered photos have this disastrous an effect, but you should be aware that cases like this do happen.

---

4 If you would like to see the original and the manipulated photos, you can find them reproduced in Alexios Mantzarlis's article about detecting fake news on *Poynter.org* (https://www.poynter.org/news/6-tips-debunk-fake-news-stories-yourself). If you would like to read more about how this situation affected Jubbal, read his article, "I Was Accused of Carrying Out the Paris Attacks" at *The Guardian.com*: https://www.theguardian.com/lifeandstyle/2016/jul/01/experience-i-was-accused-of-carrying-out-the-paris-attacks.

G. Guidelines for Evaluating Images and Using Them Ethically

When evaluating an image that you've found, consider the following:

- Who created this image? Who is the artist or photographer?
- Where was this image originally published?
- If you can't immediately answer these first two questions, try an image search on Google or another search engine.
- For what purpose was this image created? Is it intended to sell a product, support an argument, document an event, explain a process?
- What argument is conveyed through this image?
- What elements of the image contribute to (or detract from) its persuasiveness?
- Does this image include any words or complement a written text? If so, how would you describe the conjunction between the words and the image?
- Are there any signs that the image may have been altered from the original?

When incorporating another person's image into your own work, be sure to do the following:

- Give the creator credit. Include the creator's name at the bottom of your visual, and include an entry for the image on your works cited page.
  - If you're using a photograph or illustration that you've created yourself, you should give yourself credit too! Your name should appear at the bottom of the visual. If you don't do this, your audience may wonder about the source and see you as unreliable.
- Make sure you have the right to re-use the image. If you're looking for a visual to complement your text, you can go to a number of sites that provide free access to images that are in the

public domain,[5] including WikiMedia Commons and Creative Commons. The website for the Metropolitan Museum of Art also has an archive of artwork images that they have released for public domain use.

- Do not use images for which you don't know the source or creator, which is often the case for images that circulate on social media. One exception to this guideline would be an instance in which your rhetorical purpose is to show that a certain kind of image is circulating in the public.
- Place the image near the relevant text in your paper.
- Introduce the image in your text and provide enough analysis of it that your reader will understand what purpose it serves for your argument.

---

5 An image in the public domain has no copyright and is available for use by members of the public.

CHAPTER EIGHT

Using Sources to Support and Develop Your Argument

A. Introduction

B. How Professional Writers Use Sources for Research

C. Your Research Question, Your Sources, and Your Writing Anxiety

---

D. How Professional Writers Use Sources in Their Writing

E. Student Writing Sample

F. Mind the Gap

G. Chapter Recap

A. Introduction

Imagine that your instructor has just assigned a research paper. You are to choose your own topic, develop an argument about it, and incorporate material from at least five reliable sources. You're interested in self-driving vehicles, so you pick that for your topic.

What do you do next? Maybe you write a thesis statement that looks like this:

> Self-driving vehicles are safer than conventional vehicles because they take last-minute safety decisions out of the hands of distracted drivers.

Then you start looking for sources that will support this thesis statement.

If that's your process, as it has been for many of our students in the past, you are misunderstanding the purpose of research and setting yourself up for confirmation bias.

The purpose of conducting research for academic writers at all levels, from first-year undergraduates to professors, is to learn something. If you start with a thesis statement and only look for sources that will support it, you're setting artificial limits on the learning process. Unless you've already done a lot of reading about self-driving vehicles, you aren't yet involved in the academic conversation about this topic, and thus, you're not yet prepared to express an opinion about it.

B. How Professional Writers Use Sources for Research

We made this point in Chapter Five, but it's so important that it's worth repeating here and exploring at greater length: effective academic and professional writers begin with questions, not answers or arguments.

Recall Eric Klinenberg, whose work we discussed in Chapter Six. He had a sense when he started his project that many people living alone felt lonely and socially isolated. However, when he began gathering sources, through the interviews he conducted, he found the opposite. If he had formulated his thesis based on his initial instinct, he may have sought out only lonely people as interviewees. It was through his research that he discovered the thesis he develops in his book.

Like Klinenberg, Stephanie Coontz, professor of history at Ever-
green State College, experienced a change of perspective when conducting research for her book, *Marriage, A History*. This is how she
describes it in her introduction:

> This is not the book I thought I was going to write. I have
> been researching family history for thirty years, but I began
> focusing on marriage only in the mid-1990s, when reporters
> and audiences started asking me if the institution of mar-
> riage was falling apart. Many of their questions seemed to
> assume that there had been some Golden Age of Marriage in
> the past. So I initially decided to write a book debunking the
> idea that marriage was undergoing an unprecedented crisis
> and explaining that the institution of marriage had always
> been in flux. I soon changed my approach. (Coontz 1)

What led to this change? Sources. Although the historical
sources Coontz dipped into confirmed her established position
that people the world over have been lamenting the decline of marriage since the time of the ancient Greeks, they also showed that
the tenor of these complaints had changed significantly around the
time people started marrying for love instead of economic security.
Demonstrating this shift and exploring its significance became the
central aims of her book.

When Melissa began the research for her dissertation on contemporary US memoirs, she had only a broad sense of her topic.
She'd noticed that a large number of memoirs about dysfunctional
families had been published between 1990 and 2005 and that many
of them had been bestsellers. She was curious about this phenomenon and began with the question: Why are so many people, writers
and readers alike, interested in non-fictional accounts of dysfunctional families? This question motivated her to read many of these
memoirs, through which she noticed that as the narrators moved
away from their dysfunctional family dynamics, they also tended
to become economically successful. She also read research articles

and academic books on memoir, professional book reviews, and reader responses on blogs and other sites. Through reading this broadly, Melissa was able to come up with her thesis: dysfunctional family memoirs are popular because they affirm the United States' cherished myths of social mobility and the self-made individual.

Note that Melissa had no idea that this is where her research would lead when she started. She had a few other theories in mind at the beginning but remained open to other possibilities. Further, once she came up with her thesis, Melissa had to do more research, as she needed to know more about the history of the self-made individual in US culture and about the economics of social mobility.

We hope that you've gotten the sense from the three previous examples that engaging with sources for research is an iterative process. You won't be able to set limits on your topic until you've consulted a number of sources, and once you are able to set limits and formulate a thesis, you may have to seek out additional sources to support your thesis and develop your argument.

We can hear you thinking, "But I don't have that much time!"

This is true. Klinenberg interviewed hundreds of people, Coontz spent several years working on her book, and Melissa had two years to conduct research and write her dissertation. You have only the time between when you receive the assignment and the deadline, likely a few weeks. On the other hand, Klinenberg, Coontz, and Melissa were writing book-length works and you're writing an essay. You don't need to explore or cite as many sources as they did, but you must plan to use the time you have wisely. Don't procrastinate.

C. Your Research Question, Your Sources, and Your Writing Anxiety

We acknowledge that many people procrastinate because they feel anxious about a project they're about to start. That's certainly been the case for each of us at different points in our writing careers. (Yes, even professional writers experience writing anxiety sometimes!)

Perhaps the idea of starting your research without a specific thesis in mind or thinking about the number of sources you'll need to examine causes you anxiety.

One way to alleviate some of this anxiety—and make your project worth more to you than simply achieving a passing grade—is to write on a subject that you are genuinely interested in.[1] If your instructor will allow you to choose your own topic, choose one that makes you curious. You could also choose a topic that might be useful to learn about for something you want to achieve in the future. One of the students in Melissa's writing in history course, for instance, chose to write his research paper on the 1851 San Francisco fire. Why? Because he hopes to one day write a novel set in San Francisco around this time period.

If you have fewer options, because your instructor has given you a general topic that you're not very excited about, find an angle on the topic that is informed by your interests. (You'll need to find some kind of angle on the topic; otherwise, you won't be able to create an effective thesis statement, so it might as well be at least tangentially related to your interests.) In Melissa's advanced composition course, she asks her students to write a research paper on a topic related to their major discipline or the career they'll pursue after graduation. One software engineering student who was about to graduate complained; he was so tired of his software engineering courses that he'd prefer to write about anything but that.

However, in further discussion with Melissa, this student revealed he was fed up with his courses because he suspected they weren't adequately preparing him for a career in software engineering. He speculated that the reason many recent graduates weren't finding jobs was that universities weren't offering courses in the most up-to-date programming skills. Melissa encouraged him to use his frustration to fuel his paper. He came up with the following research question: how are software engineering programs preparing undergraduate students for the job market? Because he

---

1   For other suggestions on overcoming writing anxiety, see the *Who's Your Source?* website.

genuinely wanted an answer to this question, he was motivated to work on his paper.

The research question also guided him in his search for sources. Through the Bureau of Labor Statistics, he learned about the number of jobs available in this field and was able to compare that to statistics on the number of students graduating with degrees in software engineering. He interviewed several recent graduates who were on the job market, as well as a manager at a software company, who told him that recent graduates were virtually indistinguishable from one another, save for their "people skills." Through peer-reviewed sources, he learned that soft skills (another word for people skills), like being able to communicate effectively with different audiences and work well on a team, were needed in the software engineering industry, but were lacking in many job applicants. In short, this student found his motivation to complete the project, used a variety of sources to answer his question, and wrote a successful paper arguing that software engineering programs should require students to take courses that foster soft skills.

What can we learn from this example?

- Interest in a topic generates motivation to get started on a project and complete it. Professional and academic writers don't choose topics randomly; they chose topics they want to learn about.
- Beginning with an effective research question helps writers figure out what kinds of sources to look for.
- Remaining open-minded about the answer to the research question enables writers to discover the unexpected. Remember, Melissa's student had guessed the problem was that universities weren't teaching the most up-to-date programming skills, but he learned soft skills were the gateway to getting that first job. This was an eye-opening discovery for the student: he hadn't even heard the term soft skills before he started his research. Discovery is the name of the research game.

If you already know the answer to your research question, or you already have a thesis statement in mind from which you couldn't be budged even an inch, regardless of what other evidence is placed before you, you're not actually engaged in research, and your paper will sound like a diatribe as opposed to a reasoned argument.

To return to our opening hypothetical example, ask yourself, "Do self-driving vehicles interest me enough to invest a lot of time and effort in learning about them? Or, is this just the first thing that popped into my mind when the instructor announced the assignment?" If your answer to the first question is yes, then, by all means, go for it! Begin to formulate your research question. Your first try might look like this: what impact do self-driving vehicles have on the fatality rates of passengers and pedestrians?

That's a good start, but there's still a problem. What kinds of answers come from questions beginning with the word what? Usually the answers are facts. This question might lead to sources documenting the fatality rates for self-driving vehicles versus conventional cars, but then where are you going to go with your thesis and the development of your argument? Based only on these facts, your paper would be very short. You could prove your thesis statement in a couple of sentences, but there would be nothing more to develop. Remember, too, that you can't argue over a fact. (Yes, we do know some people who will argue over a fact—a few prominent politicians come to mind—but we don't view them as reliable sources.)

Try writing research questions that begin with how or why. *How* or *why* questions allow for interpretive answers. This would be a better question: how do self-driving vehicles impact the fatality rates of passengers and pedestrians?

You'd still need to find those sources that answer the *what* question, to provide the facts, but then your research question will lead you to interpret those facts. For instance, maybe you've learned through one of your sources that self-driving vehicles are associated with fewer fatalities, because they steer the car away from injuring the largest number of people. If the car has only one passenger, and there are three pedestrians in the way, the car is going to err on the side of saving the pedestrians over the passenger. Suddenly, your research question has taken on an ethical aspect. How do passengers and pedestrians feel about a vehicle making this decision based on numbers alone? This might lead you to seek out other kinds of sources, sources that deal with ethical dilemmas.

D. How Professional Writers Use Sources in Their Writing

Many of the student writers we've known have thought about sources primarily in terms of whether a source agrees or disagrees with their own points of view. This not a bad way to think about sources. You can increase your own ethos by citing experts who agree with you. In addition, when you introduce a counterpoint or two, you demonstrate that you're fair minded: you're showing you're open-minded enough to consider points of view that differ from yours and that you've done your homework. You haven't simply conducted your research in an echo chamber of other voices that harmonize with yours.

Introducing counterpoints is most effective when you can demonstrate why they are both worth noticing and also less reasonable than your own point of view or argument. You don't, however, need to give another writer a dressing down just because he disagrees with you. Remember, you are entering the ongoing conversation about your topic. You can respectfully disagree and maintain a civil tone throughout the conversation.

You should also avoid the amateur mistake of being overly critical of a writer who has written long before your arrival on the scene just because he hasn't accounted for developments that have occurred since the time that he was writing. See how skillfully Coontz handles a situation like this: "In 1975, sociobiologist E.O. Wilson drew a direct line from the male hunter marriages that he imagined had prevailed on the African savanna at the dawn of human history to the marriages he observed in the jungle of Wall Street.... But since the 1970s other researchers have poked holes in the protective theory of marriage" (36).

Coontz then follows through with a description of some of the more recent theories. Notice that she doesn't deride Wilson for his theory, but simply shows how the conversation has moved on since Wilson's time.

Depending on the topic you've chosen, you may not find sources that either agree or disagree with you. What will you do, for instance, if you've decided to write about a subject that is so new or so specific to your geographical location that no other writer has written about it yet? Give up and change your topic? We hope not! Being the first person to write about an issue actually puts you in a great position—you've found a gap in the research—but you'll have to figure out another way to use sources in your paper.

Like you, effective professional and academic writers do use sources as support or counterpoints, but they go beyond that. They also use sources to introduce an example, demonstrate why their topic is worthy of notice, document a trend, build on another writer's ideas or theories, illustrate the conversation on their topics, and locate a gap in the research. In the following, we provide you with examples of writers using sources for these purposes.

Introducing an Example

Throughout *Going Solo*, Klinenberg introduces examples, drawn from his interviews, to demonstrate that many people feel fulfilled while living alone. Here's how he uses one of those examples:

Molly moved to Boston after graduation and rented a place with roommates. She went out a lot and had a few relation-ships, but nothing serious. After six years[,] she moved to New York City, and when she could afford it got a place of her own in Kips Bay. Now Molly's thirty-seven and she doesn't think she's incomplete without a partner, even when she's

home alone. "I really love being able to create that little vac-
uum of space for myself," she says. "I don't ever feel desolate."
(Klinenberg 68)

Demonstrating Why the Topic Is Worthy of Notice

One of Melissa's students, Kelsey Klein, opened her literature
review on research concerning BRCA-gene-related breast cancer
with these sentences:

> Women in the United States have approximately an 8–10%
> lifetime risk of breast cancer, and over 240,000 cases of inva-
> sive breast cancer are predicted to be diagnosed in 2016 alone
> [1]. Women with a mutation in either the BRCA1 or BRCA2
> tumor suppressor genes, however, are estimated to have any-
> where between 37–90% lifetime risk, depending on the study
> and estimation method [2–8].[2]

By beginning with some striking statistics from her sources, Kelsey
was able to demonstrate that her topic is important and gave readers
the motivation to read her entire literature review.

Documenting a Trend

One of the points that Coontz asserts in her book is that in the
1950s, even as more middle-class women were attending universities, the general assumption was that after they married, women
would not work outside the home. She documents this thought
trend in the following way:

> At every turn, popular culture and intellectual elites alike
> discouraged women from seeing themselves as productive
> members of a society. In 1956[,] a *Life* magazine article com-
> mented that women "have minds and should use them...so

---

2   Kelsey is using the citation style of the American Medical Association;
    the numbers in brackets indicate the sources in which she found the facts
    mentioned here.

long as their primary interest is in the home." The author believed that it was good for women to have some work experience and for men to know how to dry dishes, so that they could understand and help each other. But they had to avoid "trading primary responsibilities or trying to compete with each other." Adlai Stevenson, the two-time Democratic Party candidate for president of the United States, told the all-female graduating class of Smith College that "most of you" are going to assume "the humble role of housewife," and "whether you like the idea or not just now," later on "you'll like it."[3] (Coontz 236–37)

A paragraph later, Coontz describes a survey showing that US high school students in the 1950s largely agreed with these opinions.

When a writer wants to document a trend, she needs to draw upon more than one person's opinion. If Coontz had only cited the magazine article or Stevenson's graduation speech, her readers may have rightly objected that she was supporting her assertion with only an outlier opinion.

Building on Another Writer's Ideas or Theories
In "Distracted? Work Harder!" productivity expert Chris Bailey writes:

In his book, "Flow: The Psychology of Optimal Experience," the psychologist Mihaly Csikszentmihalyi argues that we're most likely to enter into that state of total work immersion when the challenge of completing a task is roughly equal to our ability to complete it. We get bored when our skills greatly exceed the demands of our work, such as when we do mindless

---

3 Did you notice that Coontz doesn't use in-text citations for the quotations in this excerpt? Good for you if you did, but do you understand the reason why this is acceptable? Coontz was aiming her book not at an academic audience, but at general readers who might find in-text citation obtrusive. With this audience in mind, she put all of her citations in endnotes.

data entry for several hours.... Consciously taking on a greater
number of complex projects is a powerful way to enter a mental state I call hyperfocus—an attentional mode in which one
task consumes your complete attention. Your mind wanders
less often in hyperfocus because you're more engaged. (10)

Did you notice the moves that Bailey makes here? He introduces
Csikszentmihalyi's concept of flow, begins to build on it with his
example of doing data entry work, and then turns to his own concept of hyperfocus.

Illustrating the Conversation on the Topic
In "What Really Killed the Dinosaurs?" Bianca Bosker interviews
paleontologist, Gerta Keller, who, in 1978, proposed that a series
of volcanic eruptions led to the extinction of dinosaurs. Until
recently, Keller's theory has been rejected by many other scientists
who subscribe to the theory that the extinction resulted from an
asteroid crashing into the Earth. To illustrate the extent to which
the academic conversation has shuttered around the latter theory,
Bosker presents the following:

"This is nearly as close to a certainty as one can get in science," a planetary-science professor told *Time* magazine....
In the years since [the asteroid theory was proposed] impact-
ers say they have come even closer to total certainty. "I would
argue that the hypothesis has reached the level of the evolu-
tion hypothesis," says Sean Gulick, a research professor at
the University of Texas Austin.... "We have nailed it down,
the case is closed," Buck Sharpton, a geologist and scientist
emeritus at the Lunar and Planetary Institute, has said. (46)

Locating a Gap in the Research
Earlier, we stated that the purpose of research is to learn something.
To this, we now add, for academic writers, the purpose of research
is to learn something *new*, something that no one else has yet dis-

covered or written about. For this reason, academic writers look for a gap in the research. They read other sources to find out what is already known and what remains unknown, and they then craft research to address one of the unknowns.

When conducting research for a book, writing studies scholars Michele Eodice, Anne Ellen Geller, and Neal Lerner surveyed over 700 university students about what makes writing meaningful for them. Here's how they explained the significance of their findings in relation to other scholars' work:

> To date, few studies of students' writing across disciplines, especially on the scale of what we have done, have made it a concurrent goal to consider how students use (or do not use)… "funds of knowledge" (Moje et al. 2004) or how they "repurpose" out-of-school knowledge (Roozen 2009, 2010) in disciplinary learning and writing.

The authors then go on to mention several book-length studies on topics related to their own and conclude: "…but each of these monographs focuses on single institutions or even a single student and does not feature the scope and depth of data we offer" (Eodice, Geller, and Lerner 5–6). Notice that the authors emphasize the scale and the scope of their research; collecting and analyzing responses from over 700 students is one thing that differentiates their work from that of other researchers in this field.

Thinking about using sources for the purposes described above may broaden your search and help you to engage more effectively with sources, regardless of whether you are the first person to write about your topic or the 356th.

Another lesson to take from these examples is how the writers use and extrapolate from their sources. Did you notice none of them quotes extensively? Instead, they quote snippets of text and integrate them into their own sentences or forego quotation entirely and instead summarize another writer's work (as in Bailey) or cite facts drawn from sources (as in Kelsey's literature review).

In Chapter Six, we advised you not to quote too much from interviews you conduct. The same advice applies when quoting from texts. Use only the words that you need from another source to convey your point, regardless of your purpose for using the source. In Chapter Nine, we offer some tips for integrating quotations into your work.

E. Student Writing Sample

Please read Kim-Thu Pham's essay, paying special attention to how she uses sources. Can you identify where she uses them for any of the purposes described above?

Beach Cruisers at UC Davis: Living in the Slow Lane
Kim-Thu Pham

"ATTENTION INCOMING FIRST YEARS," writes an upper-classman in caps lock, "...DO NOT, UNDER ANY CIRCUM-STANCES, GET A BEACH CRUISER STYLE BIKE...trust me, PEOPLE WILL JUDGE YOU" (UC Davis Freshman Class of 2016 (official)). This quote is from one of many anti-cruiser posts on Facebook, a heavily frequented social networking site and source of popular student opinion. The blunt phrase "people will judge you" sets the tone of future bike encounters; it warns the community that one's bicycle choice affects how they are socially accepted, and it reinforces group bias against beach cruisers. On the UC Davis campus, more than anywhere else, the bike you ride sends out a message as strongly as the car you (don't) drive. Nearly 18,000 bicyclists traverse the campus daily (Lovejoy and Handy 5). The importance of bike culture in Davis means social issues surrounding bicycle choice have significant impact. The beach cruiser is owned by a minority of UC Davis students, yet this minority is still several thousand people. The stigma affects each cruiser owner by pushing him or her down the social ladder. Unique processes of social stratification arise due to the large bicyclist population. Cruiser-hate reveals that UC Davis bike culture seeks to reinforce hierarchical norms.

The unpopularity of the cruiser might be explained by its structure and functionality. Participants in the UC Davis Freshman Class of 2016 (official) Facebook group cite cruisers for "blocking the road" and being "frustrating to park next to." The beach cruiser is notorious for its large, curved frame and wide handlebars. Its speed is slower compared to other bikes, but it wasn't created to go fast. The cruiser was built for comfort. The large seat and wide handlebars support the back, encouraging a more upright, open posture. The image of the "inefficient" cruiser contrasts the faster, sleeker bicycles. Its structure is exploited in social media by people trying to make their cases against cruisers. "If you own a cruiser and it falls on its side while it was parked because you couldn't secure it properly, I automatically hate you," writes one student (UC Davis Freshman Class of 2016 (official)). A participant points out: "Hate is a strong word" (UC Davis Freshman Class of 2016 (official)). But from the twenty-nine "likes" that the original post earned, it is apparent that the student's anti-cruiser opinion garnered support. Sociologist Patricia Hill Collins's theories may explain the support for the student: "When individuals develop . . . a sense of belonging to a community, they can be more easily moved to act to defend that community's putative interests" (448). Beach cruiser owners are portrayed as violators of bike community principles. This implies that openly expressing dislike for cruiser owners is acceptable and even applauded. Within the bike community, one steps-up in status by stepping on a specific group of bikers.

Cruiser-hate serves the majority by suppressing a minority. Bike ownership indicates social worth—just as displays of wealth and fame increase one's status in society. In his article "Why We Need Things," Mihaly Csikszentmihalyi writes that power is "still symbolized by kinetic objects," such as bicycles (22). But the UC Davis bike community has changed this symbolism for the beach cruiser. It is now an object of disempowerment. Two sociologists, Felicia Pratto and Andrew L. Stewart, give reasons for the cruiser's stigmatization via social dominance theory. Social dominance theory examines group dynamics in different communities and explains how dominant groups suppress subordinate groups politically, economically, socially, and culturally. Pratto and Stewart introduce the idea of "legitimizing myths." Legitimizing myths are ideas created and spread by society; they are taken for granted because they are framed as obvious. Often these myths are hierarchy-enhancing as they reinforce the power of a dominant group by increasing social inequality. Legitimizing myths dictate how "people understand what they deserve and how they and others should be treated" (Pratto and Stewart 2). It is important to understand that legitimizing myths are not concrete—they can be shaped, changed, and completely reversed to fit the needs of the dominant group. Cruiser-hate is a legitimizing myth. Cruiser owners are depicted as nuisances to the bike community due to the size and bulk of their bicycles. However, many complaints target the alleged behaviors of cruiser owners, not their bikes. These complaints single out cruiser owners, but they can actually be applied to any type of bicyclist. The legitimizing myth tries to cover this reality by targeting only cruiser owners, thus driving group sentiment.

The common complaints about cruisers can be applied to all types of bikes. Students complain that cruiser riders get in the way of others on the road and at bike racks. The same can be said for any rider who is careless about how they bike around others. Any bicyclist, not just a cruiser rider, can bike slowly in the middle of the road during rush hour and impede traffic flow. Any type of handlebar that is improperly aligned, not just wide handlebars, at a bike rack can prevent other people from parking their bicycles. Any bike that is not carefully locked up at a bike rack can fall onto neighboring bikes. The forces of gravity do not discriminate between bikes. In a response to an inquiry on the Class of 2016 page about cruisers, one student wrote, "It's not what you ride, it's how you ride and park that earns you the death glare. Stick to the right if you're going slow; pay attention in the bike circles; don't tangle up other bikes' handlebars with your own when you park, and you'll be fine" (UC Davis Freshman Class of 2016 (official)). These physical inconveniences are not specific to cruisers. Rather, they are universal consequences of inconsiderate bicycling behavior.

Physical factors do not explain cruiser-hate; instead, we must examine the social motives behind cruiser-hate. Social dominance theory allows us to interpret cruiser-hate as a majority versus minority conflict. In college, two prominent social categorizations are sex/gender and academic seniority. Likewise, the relationship between bike choice and social categorization suggests that females and freshmen are more likely to own a cruiser. The same people who experience marginalization in the bike community also face discrimination in academia. Power objects are supposed to represent "traditional virile virtues such as strength and endurance," but the cruiser is associated with marginalized groups, which are excluded from depictions of traditional power (Csikszentmihalyi 22). This is because the beach cruiser attracts a specific group of bicyclists.

Beach cruisers are highly gendered bicycles in terms of appearance, marketing, and ownership. A casual pencil-and-paper survey of traffic around the Silo bike circle shows that 74% of cruiser riders are female. This survey was done on a weekday afternoon in the span of half an hour; over one hundred bicycles were counted. A more meticulous version of this survey would reveal slight variations, but the general conclusion is that a disproportionate number of cruiser owners are female. Cruisers are the Volkswagen Beetles of the bicycling world. Both objects have curvier and "cuter" structures than their counterparts. They also tend to come in softer colors associated with femininity. *The New York Times* article, "To Be Cute as a Bug Isn't Enough Anymore," cites Volkswagen's statistic that "women accounted for nearly 70% of buyers [of the Beetle]" (Patton). To attract more male buyers, Volkswagen redesigned the typical Beetle for "more power, less flower" by flattening the roof and elongating the body. Manufacturers relate female ownership of the VW Beetle to its physical appeal; changing the Beetle's appearance means changing its consumer base. Similarly, females may choose the cruiser because it appears girly and cute.

The cruiser is tied to the female identity—an identity that is still targeted by gendered college culture. In her presentation, "Educational Pipelines for Women," Nancy G. Leveson quotes a female PhD student in computer science who speaks about discrimination in the male-dominated field:

> I think it is very subtle, and the women who experience it have so little power to do anything about it. I can't tell you how many times I gave a suggestion...and got no response from the professor, only to have one of the nearby males in the class suggest the same thing a few moments later and be congratulated for a good suggestion. I hate this—I never forgot how much this hurt and actually came to expect it after a while.

The hostile environment for women in computer science is not a phenomenon that can be fixed by university policies; it comes from underlying social currents in an academic system that clings to patriarchal traditions. Robyn Rodriguez, an Asian American Studies professor at UC Davis, conducts a sociological experiment at the beginning of her classes.

She stands in front of her students, lined up next to her male graduate teaching assistants. Her class is then asked to identify the professor. Without fail, Rodriguez says, she is never selected. To this day, the typical image of the professor remains masculine (Rodriguez). Women are still one of many groups treated as minorities in academia. At Davis, the fact that certain females own beach cruisers simply creates another outlet for patriarchal views to manifest.

The second image associated with the beach cruiser is the UC Davis freshman. Most freshmen lack sufficient knowledge about bicycles to make informed decisions about the type they will bring to college. The cruiser excels in terms of rider ergonomics but is not built to optimize speed compared to road bikes, the more common choice for students who commute to campus. "It's one of the 'freshman!' things to do," writes a Facebook group member, "...that's because at least half of each freshman class gets [a cruiser]" (UC Davis Freshman Class of 2016 (official)). Whether or not this student's statement is accurate, it suggests that the image of the Davis freshman and the cruiser are synonymous. The stigmatized bike is associated with freshmen who are perceived as clumsy and inexperienced.

Additionally, freshmen are marginalized because of their newcomer identities. Their actions stand out in the bike community and the whole university setting. This makes them easy targets for ridicule by upperclassmen. At the beginning of every school year, upperclassmen set up lawn chairs outside the busiest bike circle on campus to watch neophyte bicyclists crash into each other. Their intentional presence worsens the public humiliation. By reinforcing cruiser-hate, upperclassmen have found new channels to reassert their control. They are able to effectively tie the image of the cruiser to the negative connotations of "freshman" status and then propagate the idea through social media. Such practices are shrugged off as introductions to campus life. However, studies show that the level of social acceptance felt by freshmen is crucially linked to their academic motivation (Freeman, Anderman, and Jensen 218); actions that separate newcomers from the college population have both negative social and academic repercussions. The cruiser stereotype also allows freshmen to shed their subordinate status by replacing their cruiser with a more accepted bicycle; they undergo a "rite of passage" into the dominant group, thus improving their social position. However, this empowerment is facilitated not by fighting for dominance but by accepting the prejudices of the dominant group. It still reinforces the group's control and therefore sustains social hierarchy.

Social processes in the bike community affecting that power distribution reveal that cruiser-hate is not just about the bike. It's about who owns the bike. What we see is not a new type of bike-based discrimination, but a reinforcement of traditional roles. Cruiser-hate points to underlying social inequalities within the college setting. The size and scope of the Davis bike community allow us to examine how outdated prejudices take new forms in a local context. Universities pose as open, equal institutions, yet this is not the case in many ways. The cruiser is more than just a whimsical bike. It symbolizes the ironic persistence of traditional discrimination at UC Davis.

Works Cited[4]

Collins, Patricia. "Social Inequality, Power, and Politics." *Journal of Speculative Philosophy* 26 (2012): 443–457. PDF.

Csikszentmihalyi, Mihaly. "Why we need things." *History from things: Essays on material culture* (1993): 20–29. PDF.

Freeman, Tierra M., Lynley H. Anderman, and Jane M. Jensen. "Sense Of Belonging In College Freshmen At The Classroom And Campus Levels." *Journal of Experimental Education* 75.3 (2007): 203–220. Academic Search Complete. Web. 12 Mar. 2014.

---

4 This essay was written using MLA 7th edition and has been formatted for *Prized Writing*.

Leveson, Nancy G. "Educational Pipeline Issues for Women." *Educational Pipeline Issues for Women.* PDF.

Lovejoy, Kristin, and Susan Handy. "Mixed Methods of Bicycle Counting for Better Cycling Statistics." [Davis] 1 Aug. 2010. PDF.

Patton, Phil. "To Be Cute as a Bug Isn't Enough Anymore." *The New York Times.* The New York Times, 21 Jan. 2012. Web. 1 Mar. 2014. <http://www.nytimes.com/2012/01/22/automobiles/ autoreviews/to-be-cute-as-a-bug-isnt-enough-anymore.html>.

Pratto, Felicia, and Andrew L. Stewart. "Social dominance theory." *The Encyclopedia of Peace Psychology* (2011). 15 Dec. 2011. PDF.

Rodriguez, Robyn. "Introduction to Asian American Studies." Haring Hall, Davis. 7 Jan. 2014. Lecture.

UC Davis Freshman Class of 2016 (official). "ATTENTION INCOMING FIRST YEARS I HAVE THE MOST IMPORTANT BIT OF ADVICE FOR YOU..." *Facebook.* Facebook, 19 March 2012. Web. 29 Jan. 2014.

UC Davis Freshman Class of 2016 (official). "Hate is a strong word." *Facebook.* Facebook, 13 October 2012. Web. 29 Jan. 2014.

UC Davis Freshman Class of 2016 (official). "If you own a cruiser and it falls on its side while it was parked because you couldn't secure it properly, I automatically hate you." *Facebook.* Facebook, 13 October 2012. Web. 29 Jan. 2014.

UC Davis Freshman Class of 2016 (official). "It's not what you ride, it's how you ride and park...." *Facebook.* Facebook, 6 August 2012. Web. 29 Jan. 2014.

UC Davis Freshman Class of 2016 (official). "...it is considered one of the 'freshman!' things to do...." *Facebook.* Facebook, 6 August 2012. Web. 29 Jan. 2014.

Did you notice that Kim-Thu doesn't cite any sources that directly agree or disagree with her thesis, "Cruiser-hate reveals that UC Davis bike culture seeks to reinforce hierarchical norms"? Many other academic writers have written about gender discrimination and social hierarchies, but none of those writers has written specifically about how those forms of discrimination have impacted Kim-Thu's specific, local concern: bike culture at the University of California, Davis. In other words, she'd found a gap in the research, but she didn't let that deter her. She went on to find sources she could use for other purposes.

Kim-Thu needed to establish early on that discrimination against beach cruiser cyclists was real. To document this trend, she turned to Facebook postings. Facebook and other social networking sites are not viewed as reliable sources, but, as you may recall from Chapter Three, less than reliable sources may be used to establish trends or to show what people are thinking. Note that Kim-Thu cites not one but five Facebook posts, because a single person's opinion is not enough to establish the existence of a trend.

She then went on to conduct her own naturalistic observation survey to lend credibility to her previous casual observation that most beach cruiser cyclists on our campus are female. Knowing that some readers might object to the idea that an object can be gendered, she drew a comparison with the Volkswagen Beetle. Some readers may accept that the beach cruiser is indeed a female-gendered object because Kim-Thu uses the car manufacturer's statistic that 70 per cent of Beetle buyers are women and its claim that it attempted to attract more male buyers by changing the shape. Why did Kim-Thu not include statistics on the gender of cruiser buyers? Perhaps those statistics are not available.

Two crucial claims in Kim-Thu's argument, that discrimination remains a prevalent problem on university campuses and that objects convey social status, warranted support from trustworthy, academic sources. For this, she drew upon psychological and sociological research, incorporating the concepts of social dominance, legitimizing myths, and power objects into her argument. Note that none of the experts who developed these concepts was specifically writing about bicycles or cyclists. Thus, Kim-Thu briefly explains these concepts, attributes them to the relevant authors, and then shows how their concepts apply to her argument. In doing so, she is using these sources to build upon their ideas.

Finally, Kim-Thu uses examples drawn from some of her sources to demonstrate the impact that discrimination can have on individuals in university settings.

F. Mind the Gap

If you've ever been on the London Underground railway, you've heard the phrase, "mind the gap." Every time the Underground train doors open in a station, a pre-recorded message, by a woman with a charming voice and accent, warns passengers to "please mind the gap." She's reminding you not to accidentally place your foot in the gaping hole between the train and the platform. Ouch! Thank you for reminding us, lady with the soothing voice.

When it comes to academic writing, we also advise you to mind the gap, but for the opposite reason. When you see a gap in the research, we want you to put your whole self (or at least your whole mind) into it.

Why? Because the gap is where original research starts. Remember our point a few pages earlier—that the purpose of research is to learn something new—something no one else has yet discovered or written about? This applies to you, too. There's no point in simply reiterating the points or arguments other writers have presented without adding any new insights or angles of your own. Further, if you find yourself closely reiterating the argument of a single author, you may be venturing into plagiarism territory.

When Melissa first learned she would be expected to be original in graduate school papers, she panicked. Me? Make an argument that no one else has ever made before? It seemed an insurmountable hurdle to her because all those acclaimed scholars had already said everything, hadn't they? She seriously wondered if she was cut out for graduate school.

Melissa now wishes that one of her instructors had told her what we are about to tell you: it's not nearly as impossible of a task as it may seem.

This is because research gaps come in all sizes. They can be as big as the one Kim-Thu encountered (no one had ever written about her specific topic) or as small as a single question that remains unresolved in the other sources that you've read (that question could even become your research question). Maybe, as you're reading your sources, you've noticed that none of them has considered a particular example or piece of evidence that comes to your mind; you think that introducing this example or evidence would significantly change the argument. There's your gap.

Further, once you delve into a number of sources, you'll get a better sense how writers handle the gap mechanically. They cite other scholars, much as Eodice, Geller, and Lerner did in the preceding example (p. 223), and then show how they're approaching the topic differently. They demonstrate that scholars Wang, Garcia, and Browne, for example, have addressed issues W, Y, and Z, but they haven't dealt with issue X. If that's the case, issue X might just be the gap that you want to slip in to.

G. Chapter Recap

Here are some tips for writing an effective research paper:

- Don't procrastinate.
- Choose a topic or angle that genuinely interests you.
- Begin with a well-formulated research question instead of a thesis statement.
- Acknowledge that finding the right sources takes a fair amount of time. Use our guidelines in Chapter Five during your search.
- Allow your research question to guide you in your search for sources.
- Remain open-minded during this process. Allow for the possibility that you will be surprised by what you learn and that your opinion may change as you read.
- Use the Three Rs approach to evaluate the sources that you find.
- Use sources for multiple purposes, not only to show who agrees or disagrees with whom.
- Mind the gap!

CHAPTER NINE

Ethical Writing Is Good Writing

A. Introduction

In August 2013, workers had to remove a quotation that had been inscribed on the Martin Luther King, Jr. Memorial in Washington, DC. The problem? The sculptor had misquoted the famed civil rights leader. The inscription had read: "I was a drum major for justice, peace and righteousness." However, King had actually said this: "Yes, if you want to say that I was a drum major, say that I was a drum major for justice. Say that I was a drum major for peace. I was a drum major for righteousness. And all of the other things will not matter."

When asked about the misquotation, the sculptor said he didn't have the space to include the entire quotation. However, his truncated "paraphrase" changed the meaning of King's words. He wasn't claiming to *be* a "drum major," but advising that if others wanted to call him that, some qualifications were required.

Commenting on this incident, Danny Heitman, a writer for *The Christian Science Monitor*, said, "It's a lesson worth remembering for authors who must use quotation in their work." That includes you. Getting a source's words right is essential in writing effectively and boosting your own ethos. And think of how much easier you have it than this sculptor. When you realize you've misquoted someone, all you have to do is delete and retype a few words. No sand-blaster required. However, to catch your mistake before it counts against you, you need to reserve time for editing and proofreading your work. In this chapter, we offer you tips on how to do so effectively.

The Nitty-Gritty on the Nit-Picky

Before we say anything else, remember this tip: cite as you go!

Too often, when we're writing, we skip the citation to keep the flow. We are convinced we'll remember it was this author instead of that author who had the quote we used in paragraph three. A few hours later, we are skimming all of the articles again, trying to find what we used.

In the draft stage, you don't have to perfect the citation, but you do need to at least drop a note to tell yourself about which author (and page number, if applicable) you used. You can perfect everything in the editing stage (which is different from the proofreading stage).

If you're rolling your eyes at the idea of an editing stage, why? Have you managed to get good grades so far by pounding out one draft and running spell check? Some of you have, for sure.

Nevertheless, there comes a time when that's not enough. If you're in our classes, that time is now. If you have a teacher who is not looking closely at citations, you might be able to get away with it for another term, but when you get into the workforce or into grad school, people expect you to know all of this. They won't teach it patiently, and they'll either tell you to bone up on your own time or to leave.

We know grad students who have been told they need to take an undergraduate class like ours (which is embarrassing) or to pay (out of their own pocket) to get their work edited (which is expensive). When Karma gets submissions for the journal she edits, she doesn't forward essays with citation mistakes to the editors for peer review. If a person who wants their writing to appear in a professional publication can't be bothered to look up how to format in MLA, Karma isn't going to fix it for her. She also sends back pieces with lots of grammar mistakes. One candidate, whose essay had so many errors that Karma doubted the editors would be able to clearly understand the argument, asked if he would definitely be published if he paid someone to fix the piece. He was disappointed to learn that turning in an essay that was generally error free was the cost of just getting in the door (and he didn't send an edited piece back).

So why are we being nit-picky? Because professional writing, in the academy and in the real world, is supposed to be clear and correct.

The bottom line is that it all goes back to ethos. If you don't get the little details right, why should we trust that you took the time to do the rest? Did you read the whole article to get the author's point right, or did you just skim for a quote? Is all the data in your chart correct?

When we have our students practice writing grants, we remind them that badly written grants aren't funded. If you can't be bothered to proofread an important document meant to get you money for your project, then why would you pay attention to details when you run the study?

A few years ago, the CEO of iFixit wrote a piece about how he makes every job applicant take a grammar test, even the programmers. He explains that there are two reasons. First, "[if] it takes someone more than 20 years to notice how to properly use 'it's,' then that's not a learning curve I'm comfortable with." Second, "[all] applicants say they're detail-oriented; I just make my employees prove it" (Weins).

Similarly, if we see a work on the works cited page that isn't cited in your paper, what's going on? Had you cited it, but then taken that paragraph out? Do you not know the rule about how you only get to put works there that you actually cited? Worse—did you forget to cite a source that you used in the essay, which means you have plagiarized?

Your audience should not have questions like this.

Other questions we'll be helping you avoid: whose words/ideas are these? Why should we trust this?

Ethos is about trust, after all—that's why ethical writing is good writing.

Pro-tip!
When you run spell-check, hit "ignore all" when spell check sees an author's name, a term in another language, etc. If the word comes up again, it doesn't mean the computer can't follow directions; it means you spelled that author's name, foreign word, etc. wrong somewhere.

B. How to Create Flow

"Flow" is a nebulous word in writing. It's often code for transitions. Thus, if you've ever been told that your writing is choppy, that it doesn't flow, your audience is saying you jump from one point to another without connection, without transitions. You might not see the problem. You know what you mean, but we don't.

Transitions are usually just a word or two. If you make a point and then start talking about your dog, the reader will be confused. If you make a point and then say "for example," and then talk about your dog, your reader knows what you're doing.

You have to transition into and out of other people's ideas when you use them. When Karma was in middle and high school, writing often felt like just stringing together a lot of great quotes, but she had to break that habit when she was actually expected to make points of her own. She needed to integrate sources.

Proper Integration

- Understand the original author's work and how it aligns with or against your own points.
- When you first start to use the source, give the full name and either what they wrote or who they are (their titles or experience [distinguished professor of X, director of the World Bank, someone who has worked in the field, someone who has lived with this disease]), in other words, why we should trust them. (You might read some technical or scientific pieces that don't set up their authors as a comparison. These pieces have usually been through extensive editing and peer review, and only valid academic sources are allowed. As a student, you have to do more work to establish ethos for your sources.)
- Integrate the author's information into your own. Quotes should not be sentences by themselves.
- Usually, you will need to talk further about that person's ideas, by showing how they relate to what you're saying. Don't just paraphrase the quote after quoting, though. That's not commentary; it's unnecessary repetition.
- Cite clearly and accurately—and whenever you use someone's ideas—not just when you quote.

Take this paragraph, from an essay Karma wrote on time travel in the *Star Trek* universe. She had just finished a paragraph about how the timeline isn't easily changed (by simply living in the past for a while), before going on to say this is in contrast to how other sci-fi stories imagine time travel:[1]

> If mere observation does not affect the timeline, then argu-ably butterflies do not either. In Ray Bradbury's 1952 story, "A Sound of Thunder," the destruction of one butterfly in the past changed everything in the future: "The stomp of your foot, on one mouse, could start an earthquake, the effects of which could shake our earth and our destinies down through Time, to their very foundation" (290). This was one of the first science fiction stories to grapple with chaos theory, now popularized in culture as "the Butterfly Effect."

Notice how confusing this would be if Karma had just written it this way:

> If mere observation does not affect the timeline, then argu-ably butterflies do not either. "The stomp of your foot, on one mouse, could start an earthquake, the effects of which could shake our earth and our destinies down through Time, to their very foundation" (Bradbury 290).

You would have to flip to the works cited page to see who Bradbury was, but you still wouldn't necessarily be able to tell from that that he was writing a sci-fi story instead of a theoretical argument about time travel. There's also no clear way that those two sentences connect together for the reader.

Don't make your reader go to your reference page to see who's talking; the reference page is for those who want to learn more about where you got your information, to find more good articles to draw from, and to check your work.

---

1   This citation uses MLA format, which is one of the most common formats for writing about literature.

C. Summary and Paraphrase versus Plagiarism

As we noted above, you have to cite whenever you refer to someone else's ideas; doing it when you quote is not enough.

Some students tell themselves that if they change the words, they're not stealing.

If you come up with a fantastic idea for an app, but your colleague takes it and changes the description into his own words and then says it's his idea, are you going to agree and let him take the credit?

We didn't think so.

There are four ways to use another person's work in your own.

1. Quoting

Only the exact words your source used can go into quotation marks; you can't put your summary or paraphrase there. Usually, we quote when the *way* someone said something is particularly striking.

If you use quotes for more than 20 per cent of your paper, your audience may wonder where your ideas are. They might also stop reading long quotes if you use too many of them. (Long quotes are generally those over four lines; each citation/essay format has a way to format them—look that up.)

Another general rule is that you should be able to discuss your quote for at least twice the length of the quote; if it's important enough to put in your essay, then you should have something to say about it. Remember, though, that paraphrasing it afterwards isn't analysis or commentary. Karma used a quote (from a Shakespeare play) in her master's thesis that was a page long, which is unusual, but she analyzed that quote for five pages. And don't throw in lots of long quotes just to make your paper longer.

What do you do if you want to use a quote, but it won't work perfectly in your essay?

Source by Olivia Norris:[2]

Imagine, if you will, that *Casablanca* had been produced as a comedy—in the original, Ilsa left Rick, the man she loved, because it was the right thing to do—he convinced her. But the comedy version would have ended with a crazy wedding, in which Rick managed to take Victer's place at the altar, while Sam played the wedding march. As Luis Gutierrez argued in his lecture in film class, "Today's romantic comedies are nothing if not unoriginal."

- Maybe the grammar is off (your source is using past, but you're using present).

In MLA, you're supposed to summarize literature in present tense, but that's not what your quote does. In a case like this, use brackets to alter the quote.[3]

Example: Olivia Norris asks us to think about what would happen if "*Casablanca* had been produced as a comedy—in the original, Ilsa [leaves] Rick, the man she [loves]" (87).

- Maybe the original author uses a word that would be unclear in your text.

Say you wanted to use the "he convinced her" part, but you realize that the audience won't know who "he" is because you haven't used Rick's name yet. Again, you can fix this with brackets.

Example: Norris continues, "it was the right thing to do— [Rick convinces] her" (87).

---

2 You won't find Olivia Norris's piece in our works cited, by the way. We made up this source.

3 Some writers don't put the whole word in brackets when they alter a quote. In other words, their text would look like this: "... the man she love[s]." Using brackets this way may adversely affect readability, so we avoid it, but it's acceptable, and some instructors and citation styles may even prefer it.

• Maybe you need to shorten the quote.

You might want to use most of Norris's paragraph, but you realize it is a bit wordy and your audience knows what happens in the original film, which means you can cut that part out. Ellipses, those three little dots you sometimes see, indicate you've taken words out.

> Example: Norris asks us to "Imagine...that *Casablanca* had been produced as a comedy...the comedy version would have ended with a crazy wedding, in which Rick [manages] to take Victer's place at the altar, while Sam [plays] the wedding march" (87).

Some writers put brackets around the ellipses. You can, and it might be good to get into the habit, but we skip them when the reader should know the ellipses are ours—Norris would have been making a mistake to put three dots there herself, after all.

• Maybe there's a quote within a quote.

If you want to quote Gutierrez's words here, what do you do? Most citation guides tell you to go read the original source and to cite that. That's a nice idea, but it's not practical. If you are using a meta-study in your argument, are you really going to go back and read every article those researchers did? What if you can't go back to the original, as in the above example? Norris attended the lecture and cites the lecture on her works cited page, but you can't put the lecture on your works cited page because you didn't hear that lecture. And you're not going to be dishonest. Thus, you will use what we call indirect citation.

> Example: Norris ends her point about *Casablanca* by citing her film professor, "Today's romantic comedies are nothing if not unoriginal" (Gutierrez qtd. in Norris 87).

You are signaling to your reader that you have Norris's text to draw on, not Gutierrez's, which is why Norris's work will appear on your works cited page.

If an indirect quote appears within another quote you're using, it might look like this: "My friend Karma's mother told her, 'If a guy can't kiss, he can't [do anything else]. Don't date him.' Karma wishes she had always followed that advice." Note the use of single quotation marks.

- Maybe there are italics in the original or you want to italicize a word to draw attention to it.

If we're reading your essay and come across a quote with italics in it, we need to know whether the original writer italicized the word/phrase, or if you did, for emphasis. Different citation styles do it in different ways. This is how it would look in MLA.

Example: Norris explains how Rick told Ilsa to leave "because it was the *right* thing to do" (87, emphasis mine).

If Norris had italicized that word, you would say, "(87, original emphasis)."

- Maybe there's an actual grammar mistake in the original.

Does the name "Victer" look weird to you? It should. The character's name is actually Victor. If your source makes a mistake, you have to deal with it. There are three ways.

a. Leave the mistake in, but signal it with [sic], which is a Latin abbreviation for "this is a mistake in the original, and I want you to notice it." We usually use [sic] when we disagree with someone we're quoting, because pointing out a mistake is a way to subtly tear down his or her ethos. In this case, you would say:

Example: Norris imagines a new ending "in which Rick managed to take Victer's [sic] place at the altar" (87).

If there are several mistakes in the sentence or if the sentence structure itself is the problem, you would put [sic] before the last quotation mark.

  b. Fix the mistake with brackets.

Example: Norris imagines a new ending "in which Rick managed to take [Victor's] place at the altar" (87).

  c. Just don't use that part of the quote.

Example: Norris imagines a new ending, with Rick taking her husband's "place at the altar" (87).

Warning: Never use brackets or ellipses in a way that changes the quote's meaning, especially since you are not allowed to take a writer's words out of context.

(We know you see people do this out in the world, that you hear news people make statements like, "can you believe that politician said, '...homeless people deserve to be homeless'?" Then you read the original statement, where the politician said, "only an idiot would think homeless people deserve to be homeless." We expect you to be honest and fair when using others' words. Set a good example for those 24-hour news networks.)

Warnings
- Don't correct a quote *and* use [sic].
- Make sure your author has actually made a mistake if you're going to [sic] them. Karma has had many American students assume that professional authors can't spell. They can spell, but they're British or Canadian. If the author keeps ending words with –ise instead of –ize, they're probably doing it on purpose. Ask Google if British English uses organ*ise*.

2. Summarizing

A summary condenses material down to essential information.

> Example: Olivia Norris says that genre fundamentally changes how story endings work; she gives an example of how *Casablanca* would have a ridiculous happy ending if it were a romantic comedy (87).

3. Paraphrasing

Paraphrasing does not condense. When you paraphrase, you put the entire idea into your own words. That's why teachers won't ask you to paraphrase an essay. You would have to give them the full essay again, but in your own words. Moreover, they must be your own words. You can't mix and match: if you use a significant word or phrase, put it in quotes within your paraphrase.

> Example: Olivia Norris asks the reader what might happen if *Casablanca* were a modern comedy. Though the real movie had Rick convincing Ilsa to go off with her husband, even though she didn't love him as much as she loved Rick, because that was the moral choice, a romantic comedy's ending would have Sam playing at a wedding where Rick and Ilsa got married, after some mishaps with Victor (Norris 87). Norris also cites her film professor's opinion that "Today's romantic comedies" are predictable (Gutierrez qtd. in Norris 87).

4. Referring to Other Works, but Not Being Specific

Sometimes you want to mention that another author has written about your topic or that you aren't going to go down a certain road, but you want to mention that another author already has. For example, Karma recently wrote a piece on *The Simpsons* and sexuality. Karma had already written about sexuality in terms of basic hetero/homosexuality ideas, so she didn't dig into that again. She also dropped a note about a chapter in a friend's book, which did a thorough job on the topic. Since her friend's name was in a footnote, his work went on the works cited page.

Referring to Norris might appear like this:

Example: *Scotland, PA* is a modern adaptation of *Macbeth*, set in 1970s America, with the fight being over a fast-food franchise. Not only is the genre different because it's a film, the director has also turned this tragedy into a black comedy. (Olivia Norris, a film blogger, discusses at length how genre changes endings [87].)

That last sentence could also be in a footnote, as we explain in our next section.

Warning

One of the most common mistakes students make is putting citations after a quote, though they go on to summarize or paraphrase. For example, a student might say, Andersen discusses why "patients are so often non-compliant" (623) when taking medications.

"When taking medications" is a paraphrase of Andersen and should be cited. If the student puts the citation after the quote, whatever comes after the quote had better not still be Andersen's idea. Since the last few words are a paraphrase, the sentence should look like this: Andersen discusses why "patients are so often non-compliant" when taking medications (623).

D. Citation Practices

This book doesn't go over any specific way to cite, both because citation practices are often updated, making handbooks obsolete quickly, and because current citation practices are available to you in many forms. If you use note-taking or citation software like Endnote, it will automatically produce a citation. As we noted in Chapter Five, however, you will need to double check that Endnote is updated, that you've used the correct genre when in-putting information, and that the spacing and indentation are correct in output.

The internet is replete with guides, though not all are up-to-date. We particularly recommend the OWL (online writing lab) at Purdue's website for looking up how to cite/format in APA, Chicago, MLA, and AMA. Note that even if you don't cite a source, you are still required to format your paper in a certain way. APA will have you put your identifying information (your name, date, etc.) on a cover page, for example, while MLA has all of that double-spaced in the upper left hand corner of the first page.

Why does any of this matter? If you know MLA, but your instructor wants APA, shouldn't you get to do what you want? If you *think* you know MLA, but you only get it half right, who cares as long as you're still citing?

We sympathize. We aren't masters of every citation style, just the most common ones in our field. Therefore, when we find ourselves asked to format in another way for a publication, we take a moment to whine before we spend time on the Purdue site learning how to re-format.

However, we still have to. Karma doesn't send along a piece to the editors if it isn't in the correct format. A candidate for publication needs to signal that he can get most of it right. If not, how can he do the more complex work of getting a piece polished enough for an academic audience?

Having a format helps you remember everything. Sometimes, students working from memory forget important details like the year an article was published. Having a format also reduces confusion. There are many times we'll be reading a student essay that mentions another source, but we can't find it on their works cited page. The student will say, "According to *The New Yorker*, . . . (45)" but *The New Yorker* isn't an author, and then we have to read through every citation before we find one that has the words "*The New Yorker*" in the middle. However, what are we to do if the student has cited several pieces that were originally in *The New Yorker*?

One student got in trouble in Karma's class because she wasn't using page numbers in her in-text citations. The student later tried to explain that there hadn't been page numbers because she read the articles online. Why the confusion? The student followed the citation format for print sources, not online sources.

Often, students leave corporate or organization authors off entirely. If there's no personal author, there is still usually an organization that is responsible for that information. When the World Health Organization (WHO), the Centers for Disease Control and Prevention (CDC), the Canadian Broadcasting Corporation (CBC), Harvard Medical School, etc. puts something out there, they are the authors.

Not sure?

Who will be sued if the information is wrong?

Thus, put the WHO (full name or acronym, but be consistent) in the author position in both the in-text *and* the end-text citation.

If you honestly don't have an author (not even a commenter name or twitter handle) then why are you citing that source? (If you are writing an essay about crazy statements anonymous people make on the internet, then you may use and cite those statements.)

Vocabulary Note

The in-text citation is the parenthetical citation in the body of the essay.

The end-text citation is the list of sources you used at the end of the document. This list has different names in different formats: Works Cited, References, Bibliography.

E. Footnotes, Endnotes, and the Rest

Karma used to edit *Prized Writing*, a publication featuring the best undergraduate writing at UC Davis. Since the essays were written for classes that required different citation styles, she didn't demand that all students use the same format in the final version, but she did want every student to fix whatever citation errors they had when polishing.

There was one essay Karma just couldn't figure out. The student was mixing and matching so many styles that Karma couldn't even tell which style the student was aiming for. So she sent an email asking which citation or essay format the student had used.

"I am using footnotes."

The student was actually using endnotes, but footnotes and endnotes are not a citation format.

So what are they?

Some citation formats, like one version of Chicago Manual of Style, do use footnotes instead of in-text citations in parentheses. However, those footnotes still have to be formatted in a strict way, and the texts are still listed on the bibliography page.

In citation formats with parenthetical in-text citations, footnotes and endnotes are not related to citation at all. Footnotes are notes at the bottom of a page; endnotes come at the end of the essay. Be consistent with which you use, and if you're publishing, see which your editor prefers.

As writers, we prefer footnotes, because they are more likely to be read. It's easy for a reader to glance down at the bottom of the page. It takes a lot of curiosity for a reader to hold their place in the essay, but skip to the end. (Many readers don't bother to do either, because they assume every footnote or endnote is a citation instead of a note.)

Footnotes and endnotes serve three purposes:

1. to insert a quick idea that would break up the flow of a paragraph, as happened a few pages ago when we said our example was using MLA format;[4]
2. to offer suggestions for further reading on a topic; and
3. to explain information that would interrupt the flow significantly if left in the main body of the essay.

---

4 Always read author Mary Roach's footnotes, especially in *Bonk*, by the way. They are hilarious.

As an example of the latter, one of Karma's students once needed to mention the average failure rate of condoms. She came up with a range after looking at 10 studies. If she had put those 10 citations in parentheses, the reader would have believed the failure rate listed was the same in each article. In her footnote, she explained that each study had a different number and she was giving the reader the aggregate number.

When There Are No Citations

Citations are always used in academic research articles. Many academic books use them too. However, some forms of non-academic sources don't use them, journalism pieces, for example. Why don't they?

Traditional journalism (with paid reporters) tends to be trustworthy because newspapers and long-form journalism magazines (*Harper's, The New Yorker, The Atlantic*) use fact-checkers. In other words, every fact, every quote is checked by someone paid to do just that.

We have to cite because we aren't paying someone to check our work.

F. Over and Underciting

Can you overcite? Not really. If you are writing a research essay when you aren't an expert on the topic, it might feel like you're citing all the time. There should be sentences where you analyze and comment, and we hope you have a thesis somewhere, but you will be citing a lot.

You could get rid of some citations, though, if you understand "common knowledge." Common knowledge doesn't mean everyone knows it; it doesn't even mean a fact is commonly known. In research, it means something that doesn't need to be cited because it's one of the most basic facts about a subject (all reasonable people agree and every single source you looked at would tell you the same fact) without citing its source. Carcinogens cause cancer. Jane Austen wrote *Pride and Prejudice*. Nggatokae is one of the Solomon Islands. You probably didn't know that last one—we didn't. However, it's one of the most basic facts about Nggatokae. Moreover, think how weird it would be to cite "According to Melissa Bender and Karma Waltonen, in their book on evaluating sources, Nggatokae is an island."

We aren't experts on the Solomon Islands, but we can sure use a map!

As you write for more and more specialized audiences, and as you become an expert in your field, you'll be better able to tell what common knowledge is. For example, if you go to medical school and then you find yourself writing to other doctors, you'll know the basic facts about anatomy, and so will your audience, so they'll trust you to talk about where the temporomandibular joint is.

When in doubt, though, just cite. You won't get in trouble for overciting.

What about underciting? Yes, you will get in trouble.

Other Ways to Get in Trouble

- Turning in the same paper to two professors. Your academic code of conduct says all work turned in to a teacher needs to be written for that class, during that term, by you.

Yes, you agreed to that. The same way we agree to update Adobe, which is to say that we agree without actually reading the contract.

If you want to double dip a paper, you have to get both professors' permission.

The same is true when you're trying to be published. Most publishers ask that you sign a statement saying you have not sent that essay to other journals (after you get rejected, you are free to try somewhere else).

- Stealing other people's papers.

We shouldn't even have to say this, but don't steal other people's work. Don't upload your partner's workshop drafts anywhere. Don't upload the handouts we give you without permission.

Karma once shared a draft of an essay she was working on with some students, to show them how editing worked in the real world.

When she sent that essay off to a journal, she got an email back accusing her of plagiarism, because a draft of that paper was on a cheat site.

One of Karma's students had uploaded it there.

G. What You Need to Look Up

Each citation and essay format is a bit different, so you will have to double check everything the first few times, until you start to remember how to do it (and then you can just single check).

Details to look up:

- How the essay should be formatted.
- How to cite multiple authors. Hint: et al. is never used for just two authors.
- How to cite when you have multiple works by the same author.
- How to handle an indirect citation.
- How to cite different genres.
- How to format a long quote (over four lines).
- How to cite dictionaries and encyclopedia entries.
- How to format different kinds of titles (e.g., book titles aren't treated the same as article titles).
- How to cite texts like poetry, Shakespeare play lines, and Bible verses.

We really like checklists, so here's one you might consider using for your citations.

- Did you set up your source fully the first time you used it?

252 WHO'S YOUR SOURCE?

- Did you use the author's last name (instead of the first name) for in-text citations after that?
- Did you format the in-text citation correctly, including the punctuation and spacing?
- Did you cite whenever you quoted, paraphrased, summarized, or referred to a work?
- Did you integrate the quotes into your sentences clearly and correctly?
- Did you explain how you were using the other person's ideas by contextualizing and/or commenting on them?
- Did you use correct verb tense?
- Did you put each work you cited (and only works you cited) on the works cited page?
- Did you order your works cited entries correctly?
- Did you use proper spacing, indentation, and punctuation on the works cited page?
- Did you format titles correctly?
- Did you make sure your works cited author matches your in-text author (i.e., if you used the acronym in one place, use it in the other)?

Works Cited

Abrams, Lyndsay. "The Case for Drinking as Much Coffee as You Like." *The Atlantic*, 30 Nov. 2017, https://www.theatlantic.com/health/archive/2012/11/the-case-for-drinking-as-much-coffee-as-you-like/265693/.

Adams, Amber. "Editorial." *Brontë Studies*, vol. 43, no. 4, 2018, pp. 271–72.

Ahrens, Wolfgang, and Iris Pigeot. *Handbook of Epidemiology.* 2nd ed., Springer Science and Business Media, 2014.

Associated Press. "Not Real News: No Jail in Canada for Misusing Gender Pronouns." *Kiro7*, 5 Apr. 2018, https://www.kiro7.com/news/not-real-news-no-jail-in-canada-for-misusing-gender-pronouns/727649542.

Attfield, Paul. "Growing Cities Struggle to Stay Green." *The Globe and Mail*, 25 May 2017, https://www.theglobeandmail.com/life/growing-cities-struggle-to-stay-green/article35107379/.

Atwood, Margaret. "Under the Thumb." *UTNE Reader*, Sept.–Oct., 1996, https://www.utne.com/arts/margaret-atwood-under-the-thumb-poetry-autobiography.

Austen, Jane. *Sense and Sensibility.* Thomas Egerton, 1811.

The Babylon Bee Staff. "'Trump Was Merely Sharing the Gospel with That Porn Star,' Explains Jim Bakker." *The Babylon Bee*, 19 Jan. 2018, https://babylonbee.com/news/trump-merely-sharing-gospel-porn-star-explains-jim-bakker.

Bailey, Chris. "Distracted? Work Harder!" *Sunday Review, The New York Times*, 26 Aug. 2018, p. 10.

Barstow, Anne Llewellyn. *Witchcraze: A New History of the European Witch Hunts.* Pandora, 1994.

Belluz, Julia. "Dark Chocolate Is Now a Health Food. Here's How That Happened." *Vox*, 20 Aug. 2018, https://www.vox.com/science-and-health/2017/10/18/15995478/chocolate-health-benefits-heart-disease.

Benjamin, Kathy. "Six Times *The Onion* Had People Completely Fooled." *Mental Floss*, 21 Mar. 2012, http://mentalfloss.com/article/30339/6-times-onion-had-people-completely-fooled.

Berger, John. *Ways of Seeing.* Penguin, 1972.

"Blame It on Lisa." *The Simpsons*, directed by Steven Dean Moore, written by Ben Bendetson, Fox, 31 Mar. 2002.

Bosker, Bianca. "What Really Killed the Dinosaurs?" *The Atlantic*, Sept. 2018, pp. 45–55.

Branswell, Helen. "Ebola Outbreak in DRC Sets Up Another Test for Experimental Treatment." *STATNews*, 3 Aug. 2018, https://www.statnews.com/2018/08/03/ebola-outbreak-in-drc-sets-up-another-test-for-experimental-treatments.

Brewer, Robert Lee, editor. *Writer's Market 2018*, 97th Annual Edition. Writer's Digest Books, 2018. Kindle Edition.

Brontë Studies Editorial Board. "Aims and Scope." *Brontë Studies*, 2018, https://www.tandfonline.com/toc/ybst20/current.

———. Table of Contents. *Brontë Studies*, vol. 43, no. 4, 2018, https://browzine.com/libraries/75/journals/36369/issues/177942608.

Butler, Octavia. "Afterword." *Bloodchild and Other Stories*, 2nd ed., Seven Stories Press, 2005.

Campbell, Stephen, and Michael Cole. *A New History of Italian Renaissance Art.* 2nd ed., Thames and Hudson, 2017.

Canadian Bureau of International Education. "The Student's Voice: National Results of the 2018 CBIE International Survey." *CBIE.ca*, 2018, https://cbie.ca/wpcontent/uploads/2018/08/Student_Voice_Report-ENG.pdf.

———. "The Students' Voice: Over 14,000 Respond to the 2018 International Student Survey." *CBIE.ca*, 21 Aug. 2018, https://

cbie.ca/the-students-voice-over-14000-respond-to-2018-international-student-survey/.

Carbon, Claus-Christian, and Vera M. Hesslinger. "On the Nature of the Background behind *Mona Lisa*." *Leonardo*, vol. 48, no. 2, 2015, pp. 183–84.

CBS News. "Wikipedia Locks Revere Page after Palin Remarks." *CBSnews.com*, 7 June 2011, https://www.cbsnews.com/news/wikipedia-locks-revere-page-after-palin-remarks/.

Centers for Disease Control and Prevention. *National Vital Statistics Report*, vol. 66, no. 6, 27 Nov. 2017, https://www.cdc.gov/nchs/data/nvsr/nvsr66/nvsr66_06.pdf.

Chung Simpson, Carolyn. *An Absent Presence: Japanese Americans in Postwar American Culture, 1945–1960*. Duke University Press, 2001.

"Citing Wikipedia." *Wikipedia: The Free Encyclopedia*. Wikimedia Foundation, 19 June 2018, https://en.wikipedia.org/wiki/Wikipedia:Citing_Wikipedia. Accessed 25 Sept. 2018.

Cohen, Matthew. "A Systematic Review of Urban Sustainability Assessment Literature." *Sustainability*, vol. 9, no. 11, 2017, pp. 1–16.

Cole, Eliot. "Outside WonderCon's White Picket Fence." *Bleeding Cool*, 6 Apr. 2017, https://www.bleedingcool.com/2017/04/06/outside-wondercons-white-picket-fence-lgbt-takes-kill-shakespeare-vision-steven-universe/.

Cook, Peter. "Review of *Elmet* by Fiona Mozley and *Ill Will: The Untold Story of Heathcliff* by Michael Stewart." *Brontë Studies*, vol. 43, no. 4, 2018, pp. 362–64.

Coontz, Stephanie. *Marriage, A History: How Love Conquered Marriage*. Penguin, 2005.

D'Agata, John, and Jim Fingal. *The Lifespan of a Fact*. W.W. Norton, 2012.

Dames, Nicholas. "Jane Austen Is Everything." *The Atlantic*, Sept. 2017, https://www.theatlantic.com/magazine/archive/2017/09/jane-austen-is-everything/534186/.

Da Vinci, Leonardo. *Mona Lisa*. 1506, Le Louvre, Paris.

"Death Taxes." *Investopedia*. 22 May 2018, https://www.investopedia.com/terms/d/death-taxes.asp.

Doody, Margaret Anne. *Jane Austen's Names: Riddles, Persons, Places*. University of Chicago Press, 2015.

"The Dragon and the Wolf." *Game of Thrones*, directed by Jeremy Podeswa, HBO, 16 July 2017.

DuBois, Gérard. Illustration for "How to Stop Overprescribing Antibiotics." *The New York Times*, 25 Mar. 2016, https://www.nytimes.com/2016/03/27/opinion/sunday/how-to-stop-over-prescribing-antibiotics.html.

Duckett, Bob. "Review of *Ill Will: The Untold Story of Heathcliff* by Michael Stewart." *Brontë Studies*, vol. 43, no. 4, 2018, pp. 360–62.

"Dying to Be Thin." *Nova*, directed by Larkin McPhee, *PBS*, 12 Dec. 2000.

Edelson, Meredyth Goldberg. "Are the Majority of Children with Autism Mentally Retarded?: A Systematic Evaluation of the Data." *Focus on Autism and Other Developmental Disabilities*, vol. 21, no. 2, Summer 2006, pp. 66–83.

Eglimez, Gokhan, et al. "Environmental Sustainability Benchmarking of the US and Canada Metropoles." *Cities*, vol. 42, 2015, pp. 31–41.

Engber, Daniel. "Bad Footnotes Can Be Deadly." *Slate*, 11 June 2017, http://www.slate.com/articles/health_and_science/science/2017/06/how_bad_footnotes_helped_cause_the_opioid_crisis.html.

———. "The Sugar Wars." *The Atlantic*, Jan. 2017, https://www.theatlantic.com/magazine/archive/2017/01/the-sugar-wars/508751/.

Eodice, Michelle, et al. *The Meaningful Writing Project*. University Press of Colorado, 2016.

"Episode 68." *Last Week Tonight with John Oliver*, written by Tim Carvell, Dan Gurewitch, and John Oliver, HBO, 17 Apr. 2016.

"Episode 131." *Last Week Tonight with John Oliver*, directed by Paul Pennolino, written by Brian Parise, HBO, 20 May 2018.

Estes, Michael Clark. "The Wikipedia War of Paul Revere and Sarah Palin." *The Atlantic*, 6 June 2011, https://www. theatlantic.com/politics/archive/2011/06/wikipedia-very-sick-sarah-palin-supporters/351471/.

Everything about English. "Home." *Everything about English for English Language Grade 12*, n.d., http://everythingaboutenglish. weebly.com/.

———. "Simple, Complex and Compound Sentences." *Everything about English for English Language Grade 12*, n.d., http:// everythingaboutenglish.weebly.com/simple-compound-and-complex-sentences.html.

Figliozzi, Miguel A., and Chawalit Tipagornwong. "Pedestrian Crosswalk Law: A Study of Traffic and Trajectory Factors That Affect Non-compliance and Stopping Distance." *Accident Analysis and Prevention*, vol. 96, 2016, pp. 169–79, https:// ppms.trec.pdx.edu/media/project_files/A_study_of_traffic_ and_trajectory_factors_that_affect_non-compliance_and_ stopping_distance.pdf.

Fox, Craig R., et al. "How to Stop Overprescribing Antibiotics." *The New York Times*, 25 Mar. 2016, https://www.nytimes. com/2016/03/27/opinion/sunday/how-to-stop-overprescribing-antibiotics.html.

Gallagher-Mackay, Kelly, and Nancy Steinhauer. "How Schools Can Stop Killing Creativity." *The Walrus*, 12 Sept. 2017, https://thewalrus.ca/how-schools-can-stop-killing-creativity/.

Gawande, Atul. *Better*. Picador, 2008.

———. *Complications*. Macmillan, 2002.

———. "Overkill." *The New Yorker*, 11 May 2015, http://www. newyorker.com/magazine/2015/05/11/overkill-atul-gawande.

Gessner, Ingrid. *From Sites of Memory to Cybersights: (Re)Framing Japanese American Experiences*. American Studies: A Monograph Series, 2007.

Goldstein, E. Bruce. *Encyclopedia of Perception*. SAGE Publications, 2011.

Government of Canada. "Canadian Antimicrobial Resistance

Surveillance System Report." *Government of Canada*, 2017, https://www.canada.ca/en/public-health/services/publications/drugs-health-products/canadian-antimicrobial-resistance-surveillance-system-2017-report-executive-summary.html.

Greenspon, Edward, and Taylor Owen. "'Fake News 2.0': A Threat to Canada's Democracy." *The Globe and Mail*, 29 May 2017, https://www.theglobeandmail.com/opinion/fake-news-20-a-threat-to-canadas-democracy/article35138104/.

Griffin, John Howard. *Black Like Me*. Houghton Mifflin, 1961.

Grinspan, Jon. "The Stephen Colbert of the Civil War." *The New York Times*, 11 June 2012, https://opinionator.blogs.nytimes.com/2012/06/11/the-stephen-colbert-of-the-civil-war-2/.

Hamblin, James. "How to Sleep." *The Atlantic*, Jan./Feb. 2017, https://www.theatlantic.com/magazine/archive/2017/01/how-to-sleep/508781/.

Heitman, Danny. "Martin Luther King, Jr. and the Danger of the Misquote." *The Christian Science Monitor*, 27 Aug. 2013, https://www.csmonitor.com/Books/chapter-and-verse/2013/0827/Martin-Luther-King-Jr.-Memorial-and-the-danger-of-the-misquote.

Ipsos. "United States Tax Policy: Ipsos Poll Conducted on Behalf of National Public Radio." *NPR*, Apr. 2017, https://apps.npr.org/documents/document.html?id=3671669-NPR-Ipsos-Tax-Poll.

Jubbal, Veerender. "I Was Accused of Carrying Out the Paris Attacks." *The Guardian*, 8 July 2016, https://www.theguardian.com/lifeandstyle/2016/jul/01/experience-i-was-accused-of-carrying-out-the-paris-attacks.

Kearny, Christine. "*New Yorker* Writer Resigns after Faking Bob Dylan Quotes." *Reuters*, 30 July 2012, https://in.reuters.com/article/entertainment-us-media-newyorker/new-yorker-writer-resigns-after-faking-bob-dylan-quotes-idINBRE86T1G520120730.

Khosravi, Robab. "Blurring Boundaries and a Generic Matrix in *Jane Eyre*'s 'Political Unconscious.'" *Brontë Studies*, vol. 43, no. 4, 2018, pp. 311–22.

Klein, Kelsey. "Non-genetic Determinants of Breast Cancer Risk in BRCA1/2 Mutation Carriers: A Review of Potential Preventative Factors." *Prized Writing 2016–2017*, edited by Gregory Miller, University of California, Davis, 2017, pp. 188–202.

Klinenberg, Eric. "Facebook Isn't Making Us Lonely." *Slate*, 19 Apr. 2012, http://www.slate.com/articles/life/culturebox/2012/04/is_facebook_making_us_lonely_no_the_atlantic_cover_story_is_wrong_.html.

———. *Going Solo: The Extraordinary Rise and Surprising Appeal of Living Alone*. Penguin, 2012.

Koeppel, Dan. *Banana: The Fate of the Fruit That Changed the World*. Penguin, 2008.

Krugman, Paul. "Fruits of Globalization." *The New York Times*, 30 Apr. 2008, https://krugman.blogs.nytimes.com/2008/04/30/fruits-of-globalization/.

Kurtzleben, Danielle. "We Asked People What They Know about Taxes. See If You Know the Answers." *All Things Considered*, NPR, 17 Apr. 2017, https://www.npr.org/2017/04/17/523960808/we-asked-people-what-they-know-about-taxes-see-if-you-know-the-answers.

Lallukka, T., et al. "Sleep and Sickness Absence: A Nationally Representative Register-based Follow-up Study." *SLEEP*, vol. 37, no. 9, 2014, pp. 1413–25.

Lehrer, Jonah. *Imagine: How Creativity Works*. Houghton Mifflin, 2012.

Levitin, Daniel J. *A Field Guide to Lies: Critical Thinking in the Information Age*. Dutton, 2016.

"Lisa the Vegetarian." *The Simpsons*, directed by David S. Cohen, written by Mark Kirkland, Fox, 15 Oct. 1995.

Locke, David Ross. "Woman's Place." *Native American Humor*, edited by James R. Aswell, Garden City Publishing Co., 1949, pp. 321–26.

The Majestic Plastic Bag. Directed by Jeremy Konner, written by Sarah May Bates and Regie Miller, 2010.

Man on a Wire. Directed by James Marsh, Discovery Films, 2008.

Mantzarlis, Alexios. "Six Tips to Debunk Fake News by Yourself." *Poynter*, 23 Nov. 2015, https://www.poynter.org/fact-checking/ 2015/6-tips-to-debunk-fake-news-stories-by-yourself/.

McKenzie, Sheena. "*Mona Lisa*: The Theft That Created a Legend." *CNN International*, 18 Nov. 2013, https://edition.cnn. com/2013/11/18/world/europe/mona-lisa-the-theft/index. html.

Meeker, Daniella, et al. "Effect of Behavioral Interventions on Inappropriate Antibiotic Prescribing among Primary Care Practices: A Randomized Clinical Trial." *JAMA*, vol. 315, no. 6, 9 Feb. 2016, pp. 562–70, https://jamanetwork.com/journals/ jama/fullarticle/2488307.

Michaelson, Jay. "The Polyamory Trap." *Salon*, 26 Jan. 2012, https://www.salon.com/2012/01/26/the_polyamory_trap/.

Monty Python. "Logician." *The Album of the Soundtrack of the Trailer of the Film Monty Python and the Holy Grail*, Arista Records, 1975.

Murphy, Ryan. "iRobot Roomba 860 Debris Extractor Cleaning/Replacement." *iFixit*, n.d., https://www.ifixit.com/ Guide/iRobot+Roomba+860+Debris+Extractor+Clean ing+-+Replacement/88302.

Mussah, V.G., et al. "Performance-based Financing Contributes to the Resilience Services Affected by the Liberian Ebola Outbreak." *Public Health Action*, vol. 17, no. 1, 2017, pp. S100–05.

Natural Intelligence. "Top 10 Best Dating Sites." 2018, https://m. top10bestdatingsites.com.

The New Yorker Staff. "Atul Gawande." *The New Yorker*, 2018, https://www.newyorker.com/contributors/atul-gawande.

Ogden, James, et al. "A Brontë Reading List: Part 9." *Brontë Studies*, vol. 43, no. 4, 2018, pp. 341–55.

Ohlheiser, Abby, and Sarah Larimer. "The Viral Story of Taiwan Jones, Who Learned He Failed His Midterms on Twitter, Doesn't Add Up." *The Washington Post*, 20 Oct. 2017, https://www.washingtonpost.com/news/the-intersect/ wp/2017/10/20/the-viral-story-of-taiwan-jones-who-learned-he-failed-his-midterms-on-twitter-doesnt-add-up/?noredirect=on&utm_term=.9536d0ce1a49.

Olsen, Kirstin. *All Things Austen: An Encyclopedia of Austen's World*. Greenwood, 2005.

The Onion Staff. "Harry Potter Sparks Rise in Satanism among Children." *The Onion*, 26 July 2000, http://www.theonion.com/article/harry-potter-books-spark-rise-in-satanism-among-ch-2413.

Othman, Neda. "Ensured Insurance." *UC Davis Health Student Review*, vol. 1, UC Davis, https://www.ucdmc.ucdavis.edu/mdprogram/review/pdfs/Othman-Neda-OPINION.pdf.

"Paul Revere." *Wikipedia, The Free Encyclopedia*. Wikimedia Foundation, 25 June 2019, https://en.wikipedia.org/w/index.php?title=Special:CiteThisPage&page=Paul_Revere&id=903379221. Accessed 7 July 2019.

Pettit, Emma. "These Professors Don't Work for Predatory Journals." *The Chronicle of Higher Education*, 1 Aug. 2018, https://www.chronicle.com/article/These-Professors-Don-t-Work/244120.

Pew Research Center. "Demographics and Political Views of News Audiences." *Pew Research Center*, 27 Sept. 2012, http://www.people-press.org/2012/09/27/section-4-demographics-and-political-views-of-news-audiences/.

Pham, Kim-Thu. "Beach Cruisers at UC Davis: Living in the Slow Lane." *Prized Writing 2013–2014*, edited by Karma Waltonen, University of California, Davis, 2014, pp. 59–66.

Pollan, Michael. "Power Steer." *The New York Times Magazine*, 31 Mar. 2002, https://www.nytimes.com/2002/03/31/magazine/power-steer.html.

Porter, Jane, and Hershel Jick. "Addiction Rare in Patients Treated with Narcotics." *New England Journal of Medicine*, vol. 302, 1980, p. 123.

Pricer, Wayne F. "At Issue: Helicopter Parents and Millennial Students, an Annotated Bibliography." *Community College Enterprise*, Nov. 2008, pp. 93–108.

Radford, Benjamin. "Anorexia Misinformation in the Media: A Case
    Study of the PBS Show 'Nova.'" *Center for Inquiry*, 18 Feb. 2015,
    https://centerforinquiry.org/blog/anorexia_misinformation_in_
    the_media_case_study_of_the_pbs_show_nova/.

Reeves, Richard. *Infamy: The Shocking Story of the Japanese
    American Internment in World War II*. Holt & Company, 2015.

Requarth, Tim. "Scientists, Stop Thinking Explaining Science
    Will Fix Things." *Slate*, 19 Apr. 2017, http://www.slate.com/
    articles/health_and_science/science/2017/04/explaining_
    science_won_t_fix_information_illiteracy.html.

Roach, Mary. *Bonk: The Curious Coupling of Science and Sex*.
    W.W. Norton & Company, 2008.

Rosenberg, David. "Pole Dancing in the Privacy of Your Own
    Home." *Slate*, 3 Apr. 2014, http://www.slate.com/blogs/
    behold/2014/04/03/tom_sanders_pole_dancing_at_home_
    looks_at_women_who_enjoy_pole_dancing_in.html.

Samir, K.C. "Human Population Stabilization." *Encyclopedia of Biodi-
    versity*, edited by Simon Levin, Elsevier Science, 2013, pp. 199–209.

Segran, Elizabeth. "Why a Fake Article Titled 'Cuckoo for Cocoa
    Puffs?' Was Accepted by 17 Medical Journals." *FastCom-
    pany*, 27 Jan. 2015, https://www.fastcompany.com/3041493/
    why-a-fake-article-cuckoo-for-cocoa-puffs-was-accepted-
    by-17-medical-journals.

Shellenberger, Sue. "Helicopter Parenting: A Breakdown." *Wall
    Street Journal Online*, 27 Sept. 2007, https://www.wsj.com/
    articles/SB119084349844440465.

Smith, Matthew. "Does Pineapple Belong on Pizza?" *YouGov*,
    6 Mar. 2017, https://yougov.co.uk/news/2017/03/06/does-
    pineapple-belong-pizza/.

The Spesh Man. "BlankMap-World-2007," *Wikimedia Com-
    mons*, 30 Mar. 2010, https://commons.wikimedia.org/wiki/
    File:BlankMap-World-2007.png.

Statista. "Per Capita Consumption of Bananas in United States
    from 2000–2016 (in Pounds)." *Statista.com*, 2018, https://
    www.statista.com/statistics/257188/per-capita-consumption-
    of-fresh-bananas-in-the-us/.

Stewart K., et al. "Understanding about Food among 6–11 Year Olds in South Wales." *Food Culture Society*, vol. 9, 2006, pp. 317–33.

Swift, Jonathan. *A Modest Proposal and Other Satirical Works*. Dover, 1996.

Thornhill, Randy, and Craig T. Palmer. *A Natural History of Rape*. MIT Press, 2000.

Trask, Randy. "Meeting the Demands of the Job Market with Education Opportunities for Frontline Workers." *Huffpost*, 12 Apr. 2017, https://www.huffingtonpost.com/entry/meeting-the-demands-of-the-job-market-with-education_us_58ee849ce4b04cae050dc413.

"Treehouse of Horror VII." *The Simpsons*, directed by Mike B. Anderson, written by Ken Keeler, Dan Greaney, and David S. Cohen, Fox, 27 Oct. 1996.

"12 Sept. 2007." *The Daily Show with Jon Stewart*, Comedy Central, 12 Sept. 2007.

United States Bureau of Labor Statistics. "State Employment and Unemployment Summary." *BLS*, 17 Aug. 2018, https://www.bls.gov/news.release/laus.nr0.htm.

van Egmond, Jeroen C., et al. "Optimal Dose of Intrathecal Isobaric Bupivacaine in Total Knee Arthroplasty." *Canadian Journal of Anesthesia/Journal canadien d'anesthésie*, vol. 65, no. 9, Sept. 2018, pp. 1004–11. *Springer Link*, https://doi.org/10.1007/s12630-018-1165-4.

Wakefield, Andrew J., et al. "Ileal-lymphoid-nodular Hyperplasia, Non-specific Colitis, and Pervasive Developmental Disorder in Children." *The Lancet*, vol. 351, no. 9103, 28 Feb. 1998, pp. 637–41, https://www.thelancet.com/journals/lancet/article/PIIS0140673697110960/fulltext?_eventId=login.

Waltonen, Karma, editor. *Margaret Atwood's Apocalypses*. Cambridge Scholars Publishing, 2015.

———. "To Boldly Go When No One Has Gone Before (or After): *Star Trek*'s Timelines." *Star Trek and History*, edited by Nancy R. Reagin, Wiley, 2013, pp. 158–75.

Weins, Kyle. "I Won't Hire People Who Use Poor Grammar. Here's Why." *Harvard Business Review*, 20 July 2012, https://hbr.org/2012/07/i-wont-hire-people-who-use-poo#disqus_thread.

Wertheim, Margaret. "Born to Rape?" *Salon*, 29 Feb. 2000, https://www.salon.com/2000/02/29/rape_15/.

Wineburg, Sam. "Howard Zinn's Anti-Textbook. *Slate*, 16 Sept. 2018, https://slate.com/human-interest/2018/09/howard-zinn-in-history-class-teachers-and-a-peoples-history-of-the-united-states.html.

Wintour, Patrick. "'Fake News': Libya Seizes on Trump Tweet to Discredit CNN Slavery Report." *The Guardian*, 28 Nov. 2017, https://www.theguardian.com/world/2017/nov/28/libya-slave-trade-cnn-report-trump-fake-news.

World Health Organization. "Antimicrobial Resistance." World Health Organization, 15 Feb. 2018, http://www.who.int/news-room/fact-sheets/detail/antimicrobial-resistance.

———. *Ebola Virus Disease: Democratic Republic of Congo, External Situation Report 16.* World Health Organization, 18 July 2018, http://apps.who.int/iris/bitstream/handle/10665/273316/SITREP_EVD_DRC_20180718-eng.pdf.

Yankovic, Weird Al. "Good Enough for Now." *Polka Party!* Scotti Brothers Records, 1986.

Young, W. Wayne. *Parent Expectations of Collegiate Teaching and Caring.* University of Nebraska-Lincoln, PhD Dissertation, 2006.

Zeeberg, Amos. "The Algorithm That Finds Connections Scientists Never See." *Discover*, 23 Aug. 2012, http://discovermagazine.com/2012/jul-aug/06-algorithm-finds-connections-scientists-never-see.

Permissions Acknowledgements

TEXT

Fox, Craig R., Jeffrey A. Linder, and Jason N. Doctor. "How to Stop Overprescribing Antibiotics," from *The New York Times*, March 3, 2016. Copyright © 2016 The New York Times Company. All rights reserved. Used under license.

The New Yorker. Biography of Atul Gawande as seen at *The New Yorker* website: https://www.newyorker.com/contributors/atul-gawande. Reprinted with the permission of Condé Nast.

Pollan, Michael. Excerpt from "Power Steer," in *The New York Times Magazine*, March 31, 2002. As seen at https://michaelpollan.com/articles-archive/power-steer/ and https://www.nytimes.com/2002/03/31/magazine/power-steer.html.

IMAGES

Los Rios Community College District Library Research Database pages:
> Reprinted with the permission of Los Rios Community College District.

The Onion website header:
Used with permission from Onion, Inc., *The Onion*. www.
theonion.com © 2019.

UC Davis library screenshot:

Index

From the Publisher

A name never says it all, but the word "Broadview" expresses a good deal of the philosophy behind our company. We are open to a broad range of academic approaches and political viewpoints. We pay attention to the broad impact book publishing and book printing has in the wider world; for some years now we have used 100% recycled paper for most titles. Our publishing program is internationally oriented and broad-ranging. Our individual titles often appeal to a broad readership too; many are of interest as much to general readers as to academics and students.

Founded in 1985, Broadview remains a fully independent company owned by its shareholders—not an imprint or subsidiary of a larger multinational.

For the most accurate information on our books (including information on pricing, editions, and formats) please visit our website at www.broadviewpress.com. Our print books and ebooks are also available for sale on our site.

broadview press
www.broadviewpress.com

This book is made of paper from well-managed FSC® - certified
forests, recycled materials, and other controlled sources.